MATRIX

OF

POWER

HOW THE WORLD HAS BEEN CONTROLLED BY POWERFUL PEOPLE WITHOUT YOUR KNOWLEDGE

Jordan Maxwell

Published 2000
The Book Tree
Escondido, CA

MATRIX OF POWER:
How The World Has Been Controlled By Powerful People Without Your Knowledge

ISBN 1-58509-120-0

©2000

JORDAN MAXWELL

THE BOOK TREE

Special thanks to Lynette and Arthur Horn for help with this project, and to Paul Tice for the final edit.

Layout and Design by Tédd St. Rain

Printed on Acid-Free Paper

Published by

The Book Tree
Post Office Box 724
Escondido, CA 92033

We provide fascinating and educational products to help awaken the public to new ideas and information that would not be available otherwise. We carry over 1100 Books, Booklets, Audio, Video, and other products on Alchemy, Alternative Medicine, Ancient America, Ancient Astronauts, Ancient Civilizations, Ancient Mysteries, Ancient Religion and Worship, Angels, Anthropology, Anti-Gravity, Archaeology, Area 51, Assyria, Astrology, Atlantis, Babylonia, Townsend Brown, Christianity, Cold Fusion, Colloidal Silver, Comparative Religions, Crop Circles, The Dead Sea Scrolls, Early History, Electromagnetics, Electro-Gravity, Egypt, Electromagnetic Smog, Michael Faraday, Fatima, The Fed, Fluoride, Free Energy, Freemasonry, Global Manipulation, The Gnostics, God, Gravity, The Great Pyramid, Gyroscopic Anti-Gravity, Healing Electromagnetics, Health Issues, Hinduism, HIV, Human Origins, Jehovah, Jesus, Jordan Maxwell, John Keely, Lemuria, Lost Cities, Lost Continents, Magick, Masonry, Mercury Poisoning, Metaphysics, Mythology, Occultism, Paganism, Pesticide Pollution, Personal Growth, The Philadelphia Experiement, Philosophy, Powerlines, Prophecy, Psychic Research, Pyramids, Rare Books, Religion, Religious Controversy, Roswell, Walter Russell, Scalar Waves, SDI, John Searle, Secret Societies, Sex Worship, Sitchin Studies, Smart Cards, Joseph Smith, Solar Power, Sovereignty, Space Travel, Spirituality, Stonehenge, Sumeria, Sun Myths, Symbolism, Tachyon Fields, Templars, Tesla, Theology, Time Travel, The Treasury, UFOs, Underground Bases, World Control, The World Grid, Zero Point Energy, and much more. Call **1 (800) 700-TREE** for our *FREEBOOK TREECATALOG* or visit our website at www.the-booktree.com for more information.

CONTENTS

For more information or to contact Jordan Maxwell directly , please address all correspondence to:

Jordan Maxwell
c/o BBC of America
19528 Ventura Blvd., PMB #449
Tarzana, California 91356

For additional information visit the related web sites at:

www.jordanmaxwell.com
or
www.bbcoa.com

Mr. Maxwell is available for speaking engagements, but due to his schedule and the great demand for his presence, it is advised to contact him well ahead of time. He also functions quite often as an MC/host for various conferences, and has hosted hundreds of his own radio programs.

PART ONE
OVERVIEW

So you see, my dear Coningsby, that the world is governed by very dif-
ferent personages from what is imagined by those who are not behind
the scenes.

—Benjamin Disraeli, first Prime Minister of England,
in his book *Coningsby*

At one time or another we've all questioned as to whether all that we see and are experiencing in our world has some sort of a rational plan behind it, because we understand now that both the Republican and Democratic Parties in America are basically run by the same people. The same money finances both sides. We now know through the work of many historians who have spent their lives working on research, that both sides of world conflicts have always been financed by the same people. And, as I've said many times before, this seems to be the method to the "madness" going on in the world. We know, of course, that we cannot depend on the truthfulness our leaders. Our leaders are "misleaders." There *is* a science they are following. They have their own agenda – and it does not include *you*.

This agenda also does not include many of our politicians, who have sometimes felt helpless and spoke out as a result. In 1922, New York City Mayor John F. Hylan said, "The real menace of our republic is this invisible government which, like a giant octopus, sprawls its slimy length over city, state and nation. Like the octopus of real life, it operates under cover of a self created screen.... At the head of this octopus are the Rockefeller Standard Oil interests and a small group of powerful banking houses generally referred to as international bankers. The little coterie of powerful international bankers virtually run the United States government for their own selfish purposes. They practically control both political parties." What I have said, however, is that they *do* control both parties, among many other things in the world.

Conflicts require money and cooperation. World conflicts require world banks and international monetary funds. Professional groups all have fraternal orders. Doctors, attorneys, etc., have their own specific fraternal orders. In the banking world, it is the same way. They have the same fraternal order in banking and politics. However, we are not supposed to know anything about that, because that's not any of our business. That fraternal order in politics and banking has been known for many years by those on the inside. It has been referred to by different names, at different times, in different countries. The best overall name that we can confer on this fraternal order, which is running our country, politics, and monetary system, is Freemasonry.

Our country, like so many before us, and like so many after us, was in fact founded by Freemasons. Freemasonry, in one form or another, has played a role in almost every government that was founded in this world. It is powerful in operation today throughout the world. However, we do want to establish first that what we are *not* talking about is Blue Masonry, or the Masonic Lodges in your hometown. We are *not* talking about the Freemasons that live across the street from you. We're talking about a worldwide fraternal organization that is powerful enough, old enough, and wise enough to operate behind all governments in the world, behind fraternal institutions, and behind international monetary systems in the world. And, yes, they are, in fact, connected.

For instance, the idea that our country was founded by so many Freemasons and Rosicrucians, among others, will be consistently revealed throughout this book. We ask ourselves, "Why do we fold the American flag in a triangle?" What does the pyramid or the triangle have to do with the American system of government on

The Freemasonic royal arch.

our dollar bill? We must now recall that our Constitution was signed in Philadelphia, Pennsylvania. Pennsylvania is referred to as the Keystone State. The reason *why* Pennsylvania is the Keystone State, is because the Freemasons that founded this country were members of the Scottish Rite. Keep following here, and you will see what becomes quite evident surrounding the classification of "keystone."

In that Scottish Rite organization there is the Royal Arch Degree. The Royal Arch Degree. And, of course, the Royal Arch, if you do not know, was originally designated because of the sun coming over the horizon in the morning, which made the royal arch. The Freemasonic Royal Arch Degree has been continually, and ever busy, throughout the world with their Freemasonic endeavors. The United States, as I've written, founded its Constitution in Philadelphia, with Pennsylvania becoming the "key stone" of a royal arch. To this day, Pennsylvania is known as the keystone state.

There is much concerning this conceptual premise in this material that we each need to look at. Who are the Freemasons? Why are Freemasonic emblems and symbols depicted on flags throughout the world, and found on all sides of global conflicts? We might ask ourselves about the Red Cross. The International Red Cross is a Masonic organization. They always, in every conflict are able to go behind enemy

A version of the royal arch – the "gateway" arch in St. Louis, Missouri.

lines. Why is the Red Cross, the International Red Cross, able to go behind enemy lines in wartime, in conflict? There is a reason. The International Red Cross, out of London, connected with the American Red Cross, comes from the Red Cross of Saint George. The cross on the British flag, the red cross – that is also from a Masonic institution.

You might want to ask yourself some very important questions about this point. For instance, why is Hollywood continually bombarding our country and this world with trash movies, which portray violence, rape, crime of every kind – a constant outpouring of appalling bloodshed? Why *does* Hollywood continue to pump out motion pictures depicting murder and violence and bloodshed? Then turning around to insist that movies don't have any influence on young people's minds, or people's minds in general, when the obvious is so conclusively true – that all tapes and movies influence people's minds. Ask yourself why. What *is* the purpose for portraying so much violence, and horror, and gory bloodshed in motion pictures? There is a reason for it. You had better *think* about it.

The Red Cross uses a Freemasonic emblem.

The red cross on the British flag is also of Masonic origin.

You might also want to ask yourself about the biological warfare going on in the world today. AIDS, coming from out of nowhere, coming into the homosexual community. Just what are homosexuals doing today, that they didn't do six thousands years ago? Why is it that all of a sudden, in the1980's, we had AIDS? Is there any connection between AIDS and Legionnaire's Disease? And, the biological experimentation going on with the CIA, the NSA, and all the other government agencies that you don't know anything about. Is it possible that there could be some sort of a biological experiments going on, some of them going awry, some of them *purposely* going awry, simply to see how far they can go. *Is* there any kind of rhyme or reason for things that are happening today?

Keep in mind, too, that what the government pays for – it gets. If you are paid to do something for the government, they will extract from you exactly what they have paid for. When we understand that, then we must look at our national universities and schools, the government financed institutions of education, to then examine the kind of students, and the level of education that's being turned out by these government financed schools. Logic will tell you that what *is* being turned out in these schools of higher education, is *not* in accord with what the state and the federal government wanted. If they were not getting what they proposed, then they would change it. The bottom line is, that the government is getting just exactly what they have ordered. They are getting just what they have paid for!

They do not want your children to be educated. They do not want you, or any of us, to *think* too much. That is why our country and our world has become so proliferated with entertainments, mass media, game shows, the distracting drivel of soap operas, the every night, inane nonsense of sit-com television shows, amusement parks, drugs, alcohol, and every other kind of entertainment. It is perpetuated primarily to keep the human mind distracted and entertained. This constant distraction assures that you don't get in the way of important people by doing too much *thinking*! You had better wake up and understand that there are people guiding your life and you don't even know it. *And*, we now understand that most all American citizens have suspected that something like this is going on. But we are all too busy being frenzied with this entertainment and distractions, trying to stay alive and live our lives, and, after all, what can one person do about it? One person can do nothing. But, a national well-informed society can do much.

Why does Hollywood do motion pictures like *Deathwish* and *Dirty Harry*, always showing how regular citizens are misused, abused, tricked and deceived by their government – and, then, one lone guy has to stand up for what's right, because the whole system is corrupt? Why do you think they make movies like that? Is there a message in that? I'll tell you why. It's very simple. First of all, these conspirators, these people, make the movies, showing you what the problem is, then they make the movies to show you what the solution is. They know that you are frustrated. They know that the people of America are frustrated, because they know there is no law and order. But, that's purposely created. We're not supposed to have law and order, *yet*! We're supposed to have crime, and the immorality, and the drugs, and the murder, and all the other things we're besieged by. We're supposed to have that. If the government did not want that, it would not be here to the degree that we have it, believe me.

The American government is the most powerful government the world has ever known. They had the ability to get a hold on Adolph Hitler a few decades ago. He had a standing army. Plus the greatest navy, air force, military, and secret underworld organizations operating throughout the world. But, this government got a hold on Adolph Hitler, because it chose to, and it wanted to. And, if you do not pay your income taxes they will find you if you go to the Amazon jungle. And, they will make an example of you. They will find you and they will deal with you, and you know it. But, for some reason they are unable to get a handle on the drugs, and the crime in the streets, for some reason. There is a reason, and that is what we want to talk about. There *is* a method to the "madness."

You might also want to ask yourself about something from the early seventies. While no one was looking, NATO, the North Atlantic Treaty Organization, changed its fatigue colors, from the dark greens, and the browns, the fatigue colors, or the camouflaged colors, to light tan. Throughout the Western world the colors would change for the military from dark greens to light tan, like sand. Why? Because this government, along with its NATO allies realized that there would be a war in an area where they would need camouflage which would be light tan. So, quietly they changed that, they changed the color, and you didn't know anything about it.

You want to ask, too, Where did the Communist government and Adolph Hitler get their money? Who financed Stalin, who financed Lenin, Trotsky, who financed the Communist revolution? You might want to ask yourself, what part did American Wall Street play, and the international bankers in New York, in Switzerland, in London? What part did they play in financing Hitler? Like the Communist movement, and God knows what else they are financing throughout the world.

The idea was that those who direct the overall conspiracy could use the differences in those two so-called ideologies [marxism/fascism/ socialism v. democracy/capitalism] *to enable them* [the Illuminati] *to divide larger and larger portions of the human race into opposing camps so that they could be armed and then brainwashed into fight - ing and destroying each other.*

—Myron Fagan

Why is it that drugs are brought into this country daily and we are not able to do anything about it? Why are we unable to do anything about the aliens pouring in across the border? I am here to tell you why. It is very simple. The government gets what it wants. There is a method to the "madness," and we are going to explain that to you.

The last two weeks of July, of every year, a secret meeting is held in our country in northern California, by the world's most powerful people. Bankers, politicians, industrialists, entertainment luminaries, a huge composite of puissant world figures. This group is directly linked with the European ruling elites, and is commonly known as the Bohemian Society. Our now famous Council of Foreign Relations, the government behind the American government, is represented at the Bohemian Grove, along with members of the Bilderberger Group of Europe. A meeting is held, once a year there, to decide on a worldwide scale a manipulative agenda concerning your future. A shining example of true democracy carried on in the dark. Obviously, here, your vote doesn't count. Appropriately, the owl was chosen as a symbol for this ilk, for it, too, is at home in the dark. The name *bohemian* carries a dictionary definition as, "Acommunity of persons who adopt manners and mores, conspicuously different from those expected, or approved of by the majority of society who disregard conventional standards of behavior." No wonder they want no input from you. More specifically, and even darker, but equally as insidious is the American organization that our own former President George Bush belongs to, namely, the Skull and Bones fraternal group supported by students studying under the auspices of Yale University. Rightly understood to be America's secretly designed establishment. The Bohemian Society, Skull and Bones, CIA, DEA, Mafia, and the IRS are just some of the groups that make up the true power behind the throne of America. Like all other kingships, America's power elite hinges on family blood. Just like the power structure of the Mafia. If you don't believe me, that an "elite" runs America, then listen to these prominent people:

Today the path of total dictatorship in the United States can be laid by strictly legal means, unseen and unheard by the Congress, the President, or the people. Outwardly we have a Constitutional govern - ment. We have, operating within our government and political system, another body representing another form of government – a bureau - cratic elite.

—Senator William Jenner, 1954

The case for government by elites is irrefutable.

—Senator William Fulbright, former chairman of the US Senate Foreign Relations Committee, stated at a 1963 symposium entitled: The Elite and the Electorate - Is Government by the People Possible?

Once again, it hinges a lot on bloodlines. The lineages of the American Presidents and their bloodlines could make an entire book of its own. Rest assured, that they are connected to the European aristocracies of power. Starting from Edward II, and the III, of England, twenty-eight out of our forty-two presidents were connected by English blood. Including President Bush and Vice President Quayle, who are also, in fact, related to each other. Most of the fourteen not connected by blood, were connected by fraternal orders used by the bloodlines, with only a few exceptions. Notably, one instance being a critical disruption by the Kennedy's, who purposefully sought to disrupt this dynasty of power in America. Owing to their vast financial backing and personal, intellectual charisma, plus much behind the scenes political maneuvering by his father, Joe Kennedy, John Fitzgerald Kennedy was inserted into the presidency. The idea being, to disrupt the status quo by establishing a Kennedy Roman Catholic dynasty, and, thereby, serving notice on the Freemasonic powers of this world of their unwillingness to coop - erate and play by the rules. Justifying feeling threatened, the established bloodlines of power in America *removed* the Kennedy threat, *twice*! Official police records showed that the John Kennedy assassination was closely preceded and followed by as many as one hundred assassinations, all of which were closely connected with the Kennedy's family rise to power.

In our discussion of secret societies, Freemasonry, and occult orders in gener- al, we want to talk about one that might be familiar to you, or, perhaps, you have even heard about. It is called the Illuminati. We don't intend to spend a lot of time on the Illuminati, but just enough to familiarize you if you've never heard of the organization.

It was founded in 1776, in the South of Germany, by a man named Adam Weishaupt. He formulated his plans in relation to the House of Rothschild in England, Germany, France, and Italy. The Rothschild banking dynasty, behind the government's of Europe, hired Adam Weishaupt to formulate a strategy for the world at that time to accomplish certain goals for those in power. That plan came to be known as the Illuminati plan. Please note that you can find most of this mate- rial in any library, any encyclopedia under the word Illuminati, which obviously comes from the word illumine, to be enlightened, to be in the light.

There is a very important book which I would like to bring to your attention, called *Fire in the Minds of Men*. It is written on the origins of the revolutionary fate. *Fire in the Minds of Men* was written by James Billington and is a profoundly important book in understanding the revolutionary radical movements of the world today, and how they were created, who finances them and what they are really all about. I would like to share with you a couple of his ideas that deal with the occult origins of the organizational arrangements on just how occult organizations throughout the world, namely secret societies, are organized. In the book, on page 87, Billington states that the story of secret societies can never be fully restructured. It has been badly neglected, even avoided one suspects, because the evidence that is available repeatedly leads us into territory equally uncongenial to modern historians in the East and the West.

In what follows, I shall attempt to show that the modern revolutionary tradition, as it came to be internationalized under Napoleon, during the Restoration, grew out of occult Freemasonry. The early organizational revolutionary ideas originated more from Pythagorean mysticism than from practical experience. Moreover, the real innovators were not so much the political activists, as much as literary intellectuals on whom German romantic thought in general, and the Bavarian Illuminati, in particular, exerted great influence. Here, Billington was specifically talking about the organization of the Bavarian Illuminati. You can't discuss the Illuminati without understanding the Jesuit order of the Catholic Church, because Adam Weishaupt himself, the founder of the Illuminati, was, in fact, a Jesuit priest. He was not *just* an ordinary Jesuit priest, however. In Bavaria he continued to support revolutionary radical thinking against the church, giving to the world what has come to be known, as the revolutionary tradition.

May 1, 1776, was when Adam Weishaupt founded this order. This date is important, of course, in the Soviet Union and other communist countries, because May 1st, May Day, is considered to be the momentous date to all communist revolutionaries, when Adam Weishaupt founded the Illuminati. This you will find, as I said, in any encyclopedia. The bait that was laid by Adam Weishaupt for control of a vast number of people worldwide, which has now become a very old and tired project. The project was called Democracy, a people's democracy. Adam Weishaupt, like many others before him, understood that Democracy has never worked, is not working now, and never will work. Basically, because of the reason, while people could be and are the central power of any government, the people do not hold the power of any government in the final analysis. And, that while on the surface Democracy seems to be the best of all possible worlds, Democracy is a very perverted form of government, because the people can be misled.

Democracy comes from the word *demos*, meaning mob – a mob in the street is a *demos*. Demos–ocracy; *ocracy* meaning rule. Demos-ocracy, or democracy, means mob rule. You might say that true democracy is like thirty-five whites hanging one black. That's democracy. The rule of the mob. Now, when we put it into more Americanized political terms, its the rule of the people. And, while that may sound good in print, the founders of democracy in our modern day form realized that the people could be manipulated into accepting whatever they would want the people to accept.

Let's go on with the subject of the Illuminati and its symbols. You will find the symbol of the secret society on the back of a one dollar bill. On the back of the one dollar bill on the left-hand side you will see the pyramid with an all-seeing eye, the eye of Horus, the Egyptian God of Light, the Egyptian God, God's son, and you will see beneath the pyramid seventeen seventy-six, spelled out in Roman Numerals, plus the words, *Annuit Coeptis*, and is translated as *Annuit*, our enterprise. *Coeptis* is translated to mean "crowned with success," or "is crowned with success," therefore, *Annuit Coeptis* is "our enterprise, which is now a success." Then in order to find out *what* enterprise was a success, read on the one dollar bill at the bottom of the pyramid, *Novus Ordo Seclorum*. Which translates as the "New Order of the World" – *The New World Order!* Now, we must remember that Germany was the home of the concept of *The New World Order.*

Adolph Hitler's entire motivation was to establish a "new world order." But, in order to establish a new world order, you have to destroy the old world order. And, that is exactly what Hitler set out to do, destroy all of the old aristocracy, familial power bases in Europe, and then set up a new world order. This brings us now to the Masonic Lodges in the South of Germany, and their connections with the French Revolution. There is a tremendous amount of information on that subject, but we won't go into that here. Suffice it to say, that there was an immense amount of Freemasonic activity involved with the French Revolution, in the Mexican Revolution and the American Revolution, and in all other revolutions going on throughout the world. There are many, many instances of Freemasons in government, Freemasons in banking, and Freemasons in fraternal orders, operating and working together, but we don't know about all of the hidden agendas. While our people were preparing to go into the Middle East, the Gulf War, we were not aware of the facts of what was *really* going on in the Middle East. That was a war designed between secret societies, factions, occult movements that we didn't know anything about. It has nothing whatsoever to do with oil, has nothing whatsoever to do with a conflict that America should be concerned with. It has to do with some very old and ancient Freemasonic strategy.

> *The world can therefore seize the opportunity* [Persian Gulf crisis] *to fulfill the long-held promise of a New World Order where diverse nations are drawn together in common cause to achieve the universal aspirations of mankind.*
>
> —George Bush, U.S. President at the time

I would like to demonstrate a point to you from this book, *Fire in the Minds of Men,* something very interesting and important, as we get into the symbols of the Illuminati and symbols of the Freemasonic orders of the world. On page 6, recounted in the Introduction, it says:

> European aristocracies transferred their lighted candles from Christian altars to Masonic lodges. The flame of occult alchemists, which had promised to turn dross into gold, reappeared at the center of new "circles" seeking to recreate a golden age: Bavarian Illuminists conspiring against the Jesuits, French Philadelphians against Napoleon, Italian charcoal burners against Hapsburgs.

Always two sides. He continued by saying that the mythic model for revolutionaries during the time of Marx and Lenin was Prometheus, who stole fire from the gods for the use of mankind. The Promethean faith of revolutionaries used the flame, or light, in a strong symbolic fashion. It was the central theme.

Here's the point. Consider a more pointed millennial assumption, that on the "new day" that was dawning, the sun would never set. Early during the French Revolution was born the "solar myth of the Revolution," suggesting that the sun was rising on a new era in which darkness would vanish forever. This image became implanted at a level of consciousness that was simultaneously interpreted as something real and would ultimately produce a new reality.

The new reality they sought was radically secular and stringently simple. The idea was not the balanced complexity of the new American Federation, but the occult simplicity of its great seal, an all-seeing eye atop a pyramid, over the words *Novus Ordo Seclorum.*

The seal that we have on the American dollar bill is an occult seal of an occult society, pursuing an occult agenda. Most are not aware of that now, however, we are hopeful that many of the people of our country will become aware of it soon. We are optimistic that books like *Fire in the Minds of Men* will help make the general population aware of the occult forces that are running their government and their lives.

It is not our purpose to spend too much time on this particular order of Freemasonry, or the Illuminati. But we do want to spend enough time so that you understand how it worked, what its purposes were and how it affects the world societies, because it is still with us today. It has taken on different forms, in different countries, but is still basically the secret ruling power in the world today.

Now, perhaps, some of you are aware of this material that we are discussing right now, and maybe you are not. But, to show that this is not just our understanding of things, we have gone as far back as the founding of the United States. We have some comments from George Washington, which we are going to share with you here. The following is an article from the Grand Jury of the State of Pennsylvania, published in the 1800's, dealing with Freemasonry and the Illuminati, and the problems they were confronting in the State of Pennsylvania.

As we said, George Washington mentioned the Illuminati, and I mentioned the Illuminati before in this book, in relation to the democratic societies that were being founded in the United States. The Democratic Party today is an outgrowth of what we call the democratic societies of Europe. The democratic societies, on the surface, sound good. But when one looks further into what democracy means and how it actually works, it does not seem to function too well. And, there's a reason.

Let me first give you an example. In the *Eleventh Report, State Investigations Committee on Education*, published in 1953 by the California State Senate, it talks about the Illuminati. If you go out and search for it, a copy can be obtained for your further investigation. In dealing with the subject of Communism and secret societies of Communism in 1953, on page 168, we will demonstrate further how important it is that you should know about, as well as study this document. It says,

> Since many intelligent persons, even those in high official positions do not appear to have acquainted themselves with the real nature and seriousness of Communism, it is perhaps appropriate to briefly provide you with some really informative, authentic data concerning it. Communism and Russia are by no means synonymous. Russia merely occupies the unfortunate position of being Communism's first victim. Communism is synonymous with world revolution and seeks the destruction of all nations, the abolition of patriotism, religion, marriage, family, private property and all political and civil liberties, concerned with the establishment of a worldwide dictatorship of the so-called proletariat, which is, in fact, an autocratic self-constituted dictatorship by a small group of self-perpetuating revolutionaries....

A bit later on page 169, the document goes on to say,

> So-called modern Communism is apparently the same hypocritical and deadly world conspiracy to destroy civilization that was founded by the secret order of Illuminati in Bavaria in May 1, 1776, and that raised its hoary head here in our colonies at critical periods before the adoption of our Federal Constitution. The world revolution conspiracy appears to have been so well organized, and ever continuing to be ever on the alert to take advantage of every opportunity presenting itself, or that the conspirators could create. It is significant in this connection that as early as 1783, when unsettled conditions and dissatisfaction in some quarters had arisen in the American colonies, subversive anonymous sermons were circulated among the colonial army to incite dissatisfaction and rebellion. George Washington immediately called the army together and in addressing them used this significant language, remembering that this is 1783. George Washington, when addressing the army, states, "My God, what can this writer have in view by recommending such measures? Can he be a friend to the army? Can he be a friend of this country? Rather, is he not an insidious foe; some emissary, perhaps, from New York...."

Then in the next paragraph, the California State Senate report continues,

> ...it is plain that George Washington believed that the then center of this secret conspiracy, so far as this country was concerned, was to be located in the city of New York....

We now know that there has been some sort of a manipulation of our government, our money, our institutions, and our lives, by our government. But what we don't realize is that there is a covert agenda. There is a method to the "madness."

We want to concertedly look into these secret movements of the world and understand how they affect us and our private lives. Now, we may not think they affect us on our private level, but they do. They affect your children in school, they affect what your children learn, they affect what you learn from daily and nightly television. There have been many movies discussing this publicly. Even George Washington in his personal letters mentions the Illuminati and Freemasonry. George Washington himself was a Freemason.

In response to a letter sent to George Washington in 1798, warning him about a Masonic movement operating in America, and this particular Masonic movement referred to as the Illuminati, George Washington responded in a letter to the person saying:

> It was not my intention to doubt that the doctrines of the Illuminati, the principles of Jacobinism, had not spread into the United States. On the contrary, no one is more truly satisfied of that fact than I am. The idea that I meant to convey was that I did not believe that the lodges of Freemasonry in this country, as societies, have endeavored to promulgate the diabolical tenets of the pernicious principles of the latter, if they are susceptible to separation, but, that individuals of them may have done it, or that the founder, or instrument founded, or the instrument employed to found the democratic societies in the United States may have had these objects in mind, and actually had the separation of the people from their government in view, is too evident to question.

What George Washington was saying was the mere fact that someone had charged that the Illuminati was operating in America. George Washington said, "On the contrary, no one is more satisfied with that fact, than I am." And then he proceeded to say that he did not believe that all Freemasons were involved in this plot, but that the founders of the democratic society in America, the Democratic Party, as we call it today in America, had the object in mind of the Illuminati's projects. "And the Democratic Party," George Washington said, "had the separation of the people from their government in view. It is too evident to be questioned." That may explain why today, in a democratic country like America, when the people make certain demands on the government, they experience no response. The people want this, the government doesn't respond. The people demand that, the government doesn't respond, because the whole concept of the democratic process in America was purposely contrived to divide the people from their government, so that the people could be out there working hard every day, taking care of their lives, feeding their children, and sending their politicians to Washington to look out for them. When the politicians got there, they were already members of certain fraternal organizations and all government was already taken care of, so that the people had nothing to say about anything. And, that's the point we're trying to make, that when you send politicians to Washington, DC, they might just as well stay home, because the rhyme and reason of government has already been decided by secret societies and fraternal orders that you don't know anything about.

In our discussion of the Illuminati we want to also, when talking about the dollar bill, and the symbol on the back of the dollar bill, share with you a pertinent accounting from the *Congressional Report*, published by the Congress of the United States. This report talks about integral steps toward a British Union, a world state, leading to international strife. International strife is very much connected with a world state, and British Union. As we revealed before, Britain is referred to as God's Kingdom, the United Kingdom. International strife, which is happening throughout the world, is part and parcel of preparing the world for God's United Kingdom, and America is playing its critical part.

God's Kingdom is, of course, coming through Britain and America. England has been chosen to sit on Jehovah's "ruling throne" until Jesus returns (according to their rules of royalty), which provides the world with a convenient racist philosophy. As I often mention, that provides the basis for racism in the world today. And then, we wonder in this country why the rest of the world doesn't seem to care for America very much.

There is a lot that we should know about concerning the symbols on the dollar bill. Let me go through another *Congressional Report*, published back in 1940. It says on page 13:

> Let me call to your attention the fact that on the reverse of the great seal of the United States, which appears on our dollar bills, you will find the exact symbol of the British/Israel World Federation. This symbol is also carried on the literature of other organizations promoting a world government, and a world religion. At the bottom of the circle surrounding the pyramid you will find the wording *Novus Ordo Seclorum*. It was this new order that was advocated by Clinton Roosevelt several hundred years ago, and recently from Philip Drew, and now followed by the Executive.

We understand now that the whole concept of a new world order is a revolutionary idea developed out of Freemasonry. I want to go back to the Introduction in the book, *Fire in the Minds of Men*, and lay the foundation for something I think you are going to find very interesting. Again, on page 6, we quote, from the Introduction:

> A recurrent mythic model for revolutionaries – early romantics, the young Marx, the Russians of Lenin's time – was Prometheus, who stole fire from the gods for the use of mankind. The Promethean faith of revolutionaries resembled in many respects the general modern belief that science would lead men out of darkness and into light.

It is interesting that in New York City, the Empire State, in Rockefeller Plaza, at the very entrance to Rockefeller Plaza is an enormous statue of Prometheus. How appropriate, and when one understands how the Soviet Communist Party was financed, organized, and directed out of New York, then it will not be any great mystery as to why in front of Rockefeller Plaza we have the figure of this Titan God, Prometheus. James Billington explains in his book, *Fire in the Minds of Men*, that that is a symbol of the world revolutionaries. Then it goes on to say in the Introduction, that there was a Millennium coming. A New World Order, a Millennium. A thousand year reign. From *Fire in the Minds of Men* it says:

> But there was also the more pointed, millennial assumption that, on the new day that was dawning, the sun would never set. Early during the French upheaval was born a "solar myth of the revolution," suggesting that the sun was rising on a new era in which darkness would vanish forever.

This whole idea of the Sun rising on a new era, a new dawn, is the Millennial assumption. We can see this openly being used today by our former President, George Bush, in such newspaper clippings identified as The New World Order, and that the world is now being formed into a New World Order. We want to talk about that, and what it means for you. The newspapers play a big part in telling us only what those in power want us to hear. You thought this was only a communist idea or concept? Think again.

> *We are grateful to The Washington Post, The New York Times, Time Magazine and other great publications whose directors have attended our meetings and respected their promises of discretion for almost forty years. It would have been impossible for us to develop our plan for the world if we had been subject to the bright lights of publicity during those years. But, the work is now much more sophisticated and*

*prepared to march towards a world government. The supranational
sovereignty of an intellectual elite and world bankers is surely prefer -
able to the national autodetermination practiced in past centuries.*

—David Rockefeller, founder of the Trilateral Commission, in an
address to a meeting of The Trilateral Commission, in June, 1991.

Control of America's newspapers goes back to the beginnings of the industrial
age, when vested interests with large sums of cash moved in.

*In March, 1915, the J.P. Morgan interests, the steel, shipbuilding, and
powder interest, and their subsidiary organizations, got together 12
men high up in the newspaper world and employed them to select the
most influential newspapers in the United States and sufficient num -
ber of them to control generally the policy of the daily press....They
found it was only necessary to purchase the control of 25 of the great -
est papers. An agreement was reached; the policy of the papers was
bought, to be paid for by the month; an editor was furnished for each
paper to properly supervise and edit information regarding the ques -
tions of preparedness, militarism, financial policies, and other things
of national and international nature considered vital to the interests of
the purchasers.*

—U.S. Congressman Oscar Callawayx, 1917

The point is, what we are being told is controlled. Controlled information. And
the New world Order idea is now starting to be presented to us. As a matter of fact,
reported previously in the daily newspaper, during early 1992, Bush urged us to
enter the Gulf War crisis. Beneath it, it says he sees the Gulf as a test of the New
World Order. That same "New World Order" is on the back of the dollar bill, it's
plainly written on the bottom of the pyramid that's on the dollar bill. That's an interesting concept, and it's one that you should know about, because what went on in
the Middle East Gulf War was part and parcel of a Freemasonic movement.

Freemasonry has made arrangements to organize and direct financial control
for different segments of society in our country and throughout the world. They
have realized that in this country black movements are moving within mainstream
America, therefore, the need arises for black leaders to be able to fall in line, to go
along, to get along. Some of the black Freemasons that *have* finally been accepted
into the order, for instance, are Jesse Jackson; Andrew Young, Mayor of Atlanta;

**The five "circles" of Freemasonic friendship: In addition to five certain coun-
tries (Italy, France, Germany, England and America), this symbol is more
recently said to represent the continents of the earth.**

Only four circles? Of course, America is not included in this project.

Kenneth Gibson, three-time Mayor of the City of Newark, New Jersey; the late Harold Washington, the Mayor of Chicago; State Senator, Julian Bond; Supreme Court Justice, Thurgood Marshall; Marion Barry, Mayor of District of Columbia. We see that Freemasonry uses all races to accomplish its objectives.

In Freemasonry in Europe the groups were called circles. The circles were called friends. There were five circle of friends, America being one of them. Italy, France, Germany, England, and America are the five circles of friends. They were called in European Freemasonry, the Olympiads, so that today the Olympiad Organization's symbol is five circles, the five Masonic circles of friends. Of course, the Audi automobile has only four circles, because America's not included in that project. The circles were, to be sure, the circle of friends within the Masonic league. The torch, of course, the Olympic torch, is the torch of Prometheus, the God who stole fire for the service of man. And, again, as we said, in New York in front of Rockefeller Plaza you will see the statue of Prometheus, holding in his hand a flame, the torch, the fire of revolution. The dime, of course, on the Mercury head dime, inscripted on the back of the dime you will find the torch of illumination. It's still there today. The modern American dime has the torch of illumination. The Statue of Liberty has the torch. Of course, on all universities and colleges we find in their symbols and emblems that they have the torches, symbolically standing for illumination of the Illuminati. As a matter of fact, when you are a graduate from a university you become an Alumni, which is taken from, obviously, Aluminati, Illuminati. Emphasizing that you become illuminated when you go to a university.

The torch is also used in the Amoco Oil logo. It is found many, many places. Chevrolet, in **The torch of illumination – the Promethean fire is a symbol of the Illuminati.**

its Saffron Division of General Motors, is putting out its illuminum car, not aluminum, but an "illumined" car from the Illuminati. Then when you go to college and a university, or even when you graduate from high school you come out processionally with a black robe, which is black for Saffron, the God of the Hebrews, requiring that you wear the square mortarboard on top of your head. The square mortarboards are, of course, used by the Freemasons for their plaster, so that is why you wear a square mortarboard when you graduate, ultimately becoming an Alumni. It all has to do with Freemasonry, it all has to do with the control of education in this country, the control of our religious thinking, our government, our money, our lives, everything. Your corner drugstore is influenced by Freemasonry, secret societies, occult orders, and politics of the scientific kind.

Our founding fathers are probably turning over in their graves as they see what has happened to us, and how we have been deflected from our purpose and our mission in the world, to ultimately become nothing but pawns in the game. Our liberty is threatened. Look at the liberty bell, the symbol of liberty. An equal identical bell was found, with the same crack, in Moscow. It's a very famous liberty bell, with the same crack. It has becomes known as a symbol, the symbol of the Brotherhood of the Bell. Bell, being Bel, the ancient God in the Mesopotamian Valley, being the one that we call Beelzebub, or Yahweh.

The Statue of Liberty shines brightly over New York, the Empire State.

There are way too many symbols, just too many things going on in our world that we are not aware of in this busy time in which we live. That incidentally, as I mentioned before, provides the basis for racism in the world today. Let us propose that it is high time we take time to look around us and see the emblems of power, see the emblems and seals of our government. Look at the dollar bill, instead of trying to earn one. Just look at one for a change, look on the front at the Masonic emblems on it, look on the back for the Masonic emblems there. Ask yourself why it is that our country operates the way it does and is there a rhyme or reason as to the way things happen.

One should understand that General Motors, Ford Motor Company, and all the other companies in the industrialized world have a specific agenda. They don't just wake up every morning and decide what they are going to do. Large, very large international corporations have to make plans for tomorrow, for next week, for next year. When you have hundreds of thousands of people on a payroll, you can't afford to wait to the last minute to decide what you are going to do. The ship of state is far too large to turn around, just overnight. It's like a giant ocean liner. The ship of state is a very large vessel. You have to make plans for it, you have to direct the people. You have to concentrate your power, you have to concentrate the people's attention on certain things, in order to get them to go in the direction for which you want them to participate. We are a very large and powerful people in America, so our masters have to direct our thinking for us and prepare us in advance for their designated plans, for their hidden agendas. And, of course, like docile sheep we just go along to get along, because we don't know anymore about it than what we see on television. It's about time that we look into this enigmatic world that we live in and examine who we are, why we are doing what we are doing, and notice just where we are going.

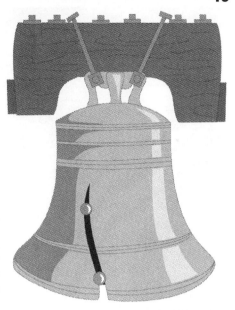

That's the purpose of what we are trying to do. As we said before, we are not trying to explain everything in detail, because we simply couldn't in this short publication. But, we are trying to make you aware that there is an enormous world of material out there that you should be concerned with and know about, and it is our purpose to provide you with that material. You will find that the many things which we have investi-

The Liberty Bell, symbol of freedom and liberty, another Masonic symbol.

gated and collected on the secret societies, on our government, governments of the world, are just fascinating.

When we remember that Abraham Lincoln was the first President to break all diplomatic ties with the Vatican, in the 1860's, we become even more aware. Diplomatic ties continued broken with the United States until the coming of President Ronald Reagan. He reestablished full diplomatic ties with the Vatican, the first President, since Lincoln, to do so. Reagan's next official act was to travel to Europe, at least three times, to meet in private with the Pope. We were not told what was discussed. Later, the Pope was a host to other summit meetings. And then, of course, Ronald Reagan traveled to Europe to visit the war dead, or so we are told. He ended up at Bitsburg Cemetery, the burial spot for the Nazi SS Officers. We have to wonder what was going on. Did Ronald Reagan not know he was going to a Nazi burial spot? Of course he did, he's not a fool. There are no such things as mistakes made by presidents. What they do and where they go is always well planned and done for a reason.

When we see things happening on the world scene, and we say the President made a mistake, the government made a mistake, you have to know that a government the size of the United States doesn't make mistakes. They are well calculated moves. They know what they are doing, and often times have a hidden agenda that they simply cannot make public. You would be amazed as to how often this happens. They have an idea, a purpose, so they don't make mistakes. Ronald Reagan's going to Bitsburg was purposely contrived. It signaled something to secret societies. The Gulf crisis, in the early 1990s, was just another calculated plan in the scheme of world agendas. There are many innuendoes, and things that are being said, which lead one to understand that there is more going on in the Middle East than what we were told about, and as we said before, it has little to nothing to do with oil, little to nothing to do with a threat against this country, because the bottom line is that this country has very little it can be threatened with. Threats certainly do exist, but not to the degree that one would think.

There are some interesting books out there which show many Freemasonic connections to our societies, religions, and political leaders, including connections

Modern clerical headwear, like this yarmulke, have their origins in the ancient Jewish headdress.

between the Order of Malta with the Pope and Rome, and the Freemasonic double-headed eagle with England. England and Rome use Freemasonic symbols at the highest religious levels, elements in relation to Christianity – or should I say Jehovah Witness's brand of Christianity. We have such books as *Christian by Degrees, Masonic Religion Revealed in the Light and the Faith of Jehovah, Testament for a New World, The Seven Books Containing a Sense of Spiritual Wisdom,* given to us by the Knights Templar. Therein, the Table of Contents reveals a Book of Jehovah and the book of Jehovah's Kingdom on Earth, with the Knights Templar emblem. We see that Jehovah's Kingdom on Earth is no more than a Masonic Kingdom, like the British United Kingdom. Jehovah Witnesses, along with the Mormons, Seventh Day Adventists and, as we said, all the other York Rite Masonic cults in America, are consistently spreading. They are the shock troops, so to speak, for Freemasonry, who spread the message for the kingdom to the rest of us in this nation to accept their Masonic Kingdom. They, unbeknownst to themselves, are the forerunners for a New World Order. However, unfortunately, they have no idea in this world, just *what* is coming. They have been duped, and they are too proud and arrogant to understand that duplicity.

We studied a book called the *Teachings of Freemasonry*, and on the book's cover we found the Jewish Star of David, because, in fact, Freemasonry is heavily Jewish. Freemasonry has always known that its greatest enemy in Western Civilization is Rome. That's why there has always been this animosity between the Catholic Church and Judaism. There has always been this animosity between the Catholic Church and Judaism. For centuries, the Jews have been persecuted in the Old Country, in Europe, and there still remains that animosity between Judaism and the Catholic movement today, but not because of religion, but because of the secret societies that operate behind the scenes of both of those organizations.

You might be interested to know that the Pope's headdress, the Papal headdress, actually goes back to an ancient Jewish headdress. And, of course, the Pope wears the yarmulke, and the highly ordained Catholic Cardinals wear the yarmulke. But, notice in particular, that the Pope and clergy wear a headdress that is Freemasonic. The breastplate and/or apron are also frequently associated with freemasonry. We have other Masonic garb showing that when we see the Pope and we see the priest, we now know that when we see other religious movements throughout the world, their garb – it's all representative of Freemasonry.

I think some of those now among us that are concerned with the race issue throughout the world might be interested to know that there is another Freemasonic brotherhood of power, which is presented as an expose of the secret Afrikaner Brotherhood. So when we see what is happening in South Africa, it is no great wonder that South Africa's greatest friend is Israel.

There is a famous song from the 1960's, entitled, *Does Anyone Know What Time It Is*? We respectfully submit that it is *time* to wake up and face the most serious problems that we face as a free society. It is high time, like the owl, that we see things that have been kept in the dark from us. This will not be difficult, because the truth has been hiding in plain view all along.

In the Congress resides the American symbols of power, known in the dictionary as the fasces. The fasces itself is nothing more than an ancient symbol, of an ancient priesthood, from an ancient world. The ax explains why, in the Second World War, the powers of Hitler were called the Axis Powers. The fasces was used by the

The Jewish breastplate and Papal headdress are associated with modern Freemasonic symbolism.

Priesthood of the Ax in the ancient world and by Adolph Hitler, General Franco, and Mussolini, and many other underworld fascist movements, likened to Mafia-style organizations, commonly understood to be called the "Untouchables."

As I said previously, and as even *Time Magazine* has obviously had to admit, our leaders are the best that money can buy. They have sold you out to a hidden agenda covertly kept behind the scenes from a long time ago. Now, you have just seen the faint outline. In the past, we have tried to enlighten your mind to a subject that has not been adequately dealt with, and that is the secret societies and subversive movements that are restructuring our world, by using all sorts of guises and

The fasces (symbol for world fascism) is represented by a bundle of sticks as a handle made into an ax.

The fasces, prominently displayed in the House Of Representatives, Washington, D.C. (District of Columbia)

excuses for their subterfusive profiles. Everything from the Jehovah Witnesses, to the Mormons, with their Zion National Park, and the New World Order, the racist philosophies that pervade the Western World. It has imminently become an idea whose time has come to speak of these subjects.

We have adequate documentation for the revelations exposed in this book, if you would like to inquire further for corroboration of this mountain of evidence. It is obvious that such a vastly controlled volume of research cannot be adequately covered in this modest edition. We do sincerely hope that we can present some of these broader concepts and ideas that could be fresh and new for you to explore. We at least want to impress on you this thought. This country was based on the premise that individual citizens have a right to know the truth, as well as the right to understand and to expect from our leaders to exemplify the truth. We haven't received the truth from our leaders, and it now appears conclusive that we are not going to be guaranteed that unalienable right as American citizens. They have their own agenda, and their own ideas about what they are going to do to continue this world control and domination, and it apparently doesn't include the opinions of you, me, or our next door neighbors. All that you are expected to do is work hard and pay your taxes, be a capital product for their controlled system, and not ever ask any questions! I think it is now high time that our country does ask questions of its leaders – its "misleaders." As I have stated before, we have the best religious and political leaders that money can buy. It is definitely time we begin to look at these subjects very deeply.

Churches, almost all churches that you will go to have a pointed arch, the stained windows, or the pointed doors. Now, the pointed arch is because of the female, that's the female womb. That is why for a couple of thousand years now, Christian priests have always been officiating. They have always been in charge, after walking through those doors, and they don't want women priests because it doesn't look right for a women to be "in" a women. It has to do with sex, and that's why the pointed door on the church has to do with the pointed arch of the female. And, the man is said to be dominating, or ruling over, commanding the pointed arch. He enters into the pointed arch, and at that time is referred to in the ancient Hebrew as the holy of holies. The holy of holies was always considered to be the womb, the holy arch, and that's where life comes from, and that's as close to God as you are going to get. Therefore, the sex act was considered to be the closest way that man and woman could get to God. It doesn't have a thing to do with being holy, it has to do with life and the female womb.

The priest wears the long black robe, because he is wearing the garb of the woman, the long black robe of the female.

The pointed arch, seen inside many churches, represents the female womb.

It was always considered, from ancient times, that all Divine wisdom was in the women, the female. She was called Sophia, which meant *wisdom* to the Greeks. Another female word is nun. In Hebrew the word nun is for fish, and there were people in the Bible like Joshua, the son of nun, and also Jesus, son of the fish. So there were men connected with this nun/fish meaning in the Bible. In many cases, Yahweh, or Jehovah, was an hermaphrodite – the God of the Hebrews was both male and female. That's what the Hebrew word for the Tetragrammaton implied, that's why the Bible says that God made man in His own image, "made He male and female," because God *was* male and female.

The seven candle lamp stand was the seven lights of the ancient world. A candle is a light. It is not a big light, but a little

Female symbolism is often found in the windows of churches because they are openings.

Churches traditionally have an arched entryway, representing the female, which the priest enters into.

---

light, that is why you had seven lights in the heavens. The seven polestars, the seven great Gods of the ancient world, in the heavens. Today we hear that God is love, but God is not "Jove." Somewhere along the line the "J" got changed to "L," now God is Love. Originally, God was Jove. Our system of numbering in America goes to ten and stops, because ten is the holy number. The holy number in ancient Egyptian, the number of God, was IO. The letter I, and the letter O. Today we have IO – the number ten, which is the highest unit you can go to, so it has nothing to do with God, it has to do with Egypt.

Our culture and our country today has its connections with England. England's royal family comes from the original Egyptian divinities, which were Isis, Osiris, and Horus. Those three divinities were called the holy family, or the royal family, and of course, today, we have the royal family in England. Believe it or not, that's where their royalty comes from – black Africa – but we don't talk about that publicly because we don't want to bring this subject up. That royal family in England gets their lineage, and there so-called royalty from actual divinities in Egypt. When you strip it all down, you are going to find out that there is nothing royal about England. I love England, and I love the English people, I am just telling you what my investigation has revealed through years of study, from books, and other academic sources.

The words Brit – ish, in Hebrew, mean a contract, or writ, a holy writ. So the word for Brit is contract, or covenant. And the word in Hebrew for man is ish; therefore Brit – ish is the covenant man, or holy man. That is where we get the idea that the King of England is so holy, because he is Brit – ish, or a "holy man." But that is Hebrew. Then when you find out where this whole idea of the holiness came from, and believe me, this is considered a very serious thing, because the King of England is considered to be one of the holiest men in the world. When you understand, then there is something that you will want to watch. And that is when Prince Charles or Andrew or whoever is crowned King, the Archbishop of Canterbury will read his initiation rites to the King, to the young man, and he will recite his rites back. When he is given those initiation rites to be King, listen to the words that the Archbishop of Canterbury says to that new King. He is saying something, and I am paraphrasing, something to the effect that "you are accepting this position as the King of England for Jehovah. You are sitting on the throne of David. And this is Jehovah's throne, God's kingdom, therefore, you are the Messiah over the United Kingdom – God's united kingdom." Now, to truly understand God's "united kingdom," (and we're talking about the Kingdom of God), we must go back to Egypt. Now, we have some serious problems here.

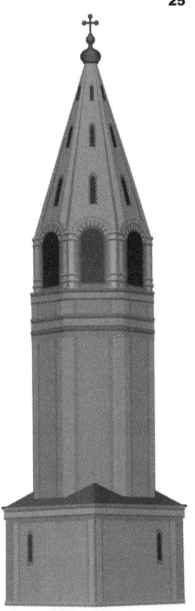

The steeple has been an object of phallic worship since ancient times.

The United States government is being ruled from the "White House," the government of England is being ruled from what is called "Whitehall," and Whitehall, like our White House, is the symbol of power because the hall is like the Masonic hall, the lodge hall, the union hall. For Jehovah's Witnesses it is the Kingdom Hall, and it is the Kingdom because Jehovah's Witnesses, like their Mormon brothers, the Seventh Day Adventist, Christadelphians, World Wide Church of God, all of those groups are British Israelite Masonic cults. Organized, directed and financed by

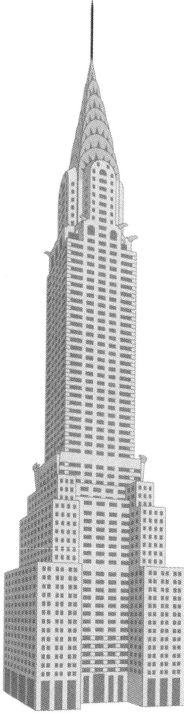

The Empire State building, representing the power and strength of America, is yet another phallic symbol.

Freemasons of the York Rite class. Freemasonry gave birth to the Mormon Church, Seventh Day Adventist, Christadelphians, Jehovah's Witnesses, and a host of other cults and groups which can be considered to be British Israel Masonic cults, who are going about telling everyone that there is going to be a new kingdom and a New World Order, and that white folks are going to rule the world. That's why the blacks are not looked upon very highly in the Mormon Church, or anywhere else in America, because this is a white man's country. It has to do with where we come from in England, and with God's kingdom and the United Kingdom, and the kingdom that is coming is going to be ruled by white men.

This is the ideology coming through the New World Order, coming through the secret societies, taking from the ancient religions and implementing their diabolical agendas, through the secret societies, through the various religious sects. The shock troupes, and the people who are introduced to the Masonic Order, the religious groups are given the out of cover of Jesus, and the wonderful story. What you don't know is that this is just a story that is actually being used to dupe and distract you from the truth. The whole New World Order agenda is being used as a front for a very sinister movement in the world, for world domination. It doesn't have a thing to do with anything holy, it has to do with politics.

There are some very powerful families fighting to see who is going to own you, that's about what it amounts to, who is going to own you and your families. There is violent philosophy in Rome, as they want to continue their world domination from the old world, in opposition to the New World Order. We have New York, the Empire State (like the Roman Empire), and the United Nations is based in New York. Freemasonry, once it is totally disassembled, and you look at all the parts, is nothing more than eclectic Judaism. It is a form of Judaism, it is not Judaism at all, but a form of Judaism that using Judaic symbols and emblems. So, it is not actually Jewish, but is *based* on the old cabalistic Jewish system.

Again, I want to overemphasize here, that I am not talking about the regular, normal Freemasonry here – please keep this upper most in your mind – all the Masons I know are fine people. I am not talking about the Masons that you live next door to. I am talking about a very secret occult society that rules this world from behind the scenes. And, as I have said many times before, don't look at the Mafia for being evil. You had better look at the real criminals, the real criminals are the ones you are never going to see. You are never going to see them, hear them, or have anything to do with them directly. They are so deeply embedded in the ancient world, and in the modern day world you will never know who they are. You can get a taste of that from the movie JFK, but that doesn't even begin to tell the story. Many conflicts going on today in the Middle East have to do with the Masonic Order, as King Hussein of Jordan is heavily into the Masonic Order. One of the groups is called the Cedars of Lebanon. It is a Masonic group. We have a hospital in Los Angeles called the Cedars of Lebanon. In the Middle East there is a secret society called the Cedars of Lebanon. It has nothing to do with those pretty trees, it has to do with a secret group of men called the Cedars of Lebanon.

Somebody is using us. The business of banking was set up in the year 1099. An income tax form is a 1099. Who decided on that? Think about it.

What can we do about this?

William Randolph Hearst, the American newspaper publisher, said, "Any man who has

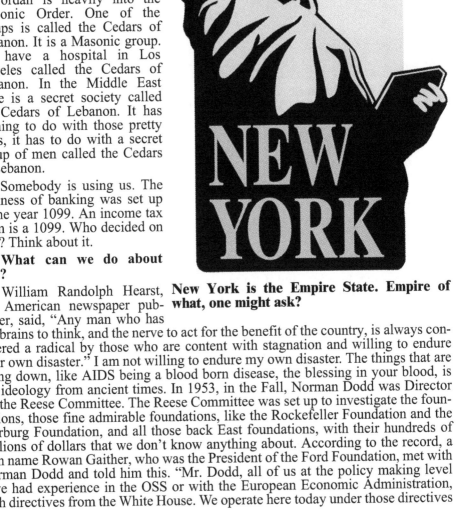

New York is the Empire State. Empire of what, one might ask?

the brains to think, and the nerve to act for the benefit of the country, is always considered a radical by those who are content with stagnation and willing to endure their own disaster." I am not willing to endure my own disaster. The things that are going down, like AIDS being a blood born disease, the blessing in your blood, is the ideology from ancient times. In 1953, in the Fall, Norman Dodd was Director for the Reese Committee. The Reese Committee was set up to investigate the foundations, those fine admirable foundations, like the Rockefeller Foundation and the Warburg Foundation, and all those back East foundations, with their hundreds of millions of dollars that we don't know anything about. According to the record, a man name Rowan Gaither, who was the President of the Ford Foundation, met with Norman Dodd and told him this. "Mr. Dodd, all of us at the policy making level have had experience in the OSS or with the European Economic Administration, with directives from the White House. We operate here today under those directives

A cardinal of the Catholic Church meets with Adolph Hitler. Germany kept friendly relations with the Vatican throughout World War II.

---

from the White House." When he was asked by Mr. Dodd, "What directives have you been operating under?" President Gaither replied, "The substance of those directives as foundations, were that we shall use our grant making powers to so alter our United States so that we can be comfortably merged with the Soviet Union in the near future." Is there something going on here that we don't know about, in this New World Order?

I would like to advise the reader to understand what we are not doing. We are not trying to put down anyone's faith, or religion, what we are trying to do is get to the bottom of what we are dealing with in the world today. If whatever we believe is not true, then we had better find out and get to the bottom line, because we are all on this planet together, and if we are part of something that isn't true, it would behoove us to find out about it now. That is what I am hoping to be able to accomplish.

In 1959 I began a study of religio-political philosophy, which turned into a lifetime of investigative research into this subject. When I was just a little kid a member of my family was a part of the team at the Vatican in the Vatican's Secretary of State Office. And, on occasion, when he would come to the United States to visit our family he would sit and talk for hours about all of the intrigue going on concerning world affairs of state. So, as a little kid I was hearing this kind of material about the fascinating subjects related to secret societies and fraternal orders.

I know a lot of people don't know very much about the Vatican. The Vatican is a country unto itself. A very powerful country, politically speaking. Heads of State from all over the world come to the Vatican to pay homage to the Papacy. The Papacy plays a very, very important role in international politics and it has always been able to demonstrate this immense power in world affairs. However, what is most interesting, is that a new development has been emerging that concerns an

Hitler meeting with the arch bishop of Germany. The politics of war required the cooperation of religion. Hitler opposed the Jews, but note the Papal headdress.

occult Freemasonic order, operating under the name of P-2, or Propaganda Due. It is made up of some of the most profoundly significant, right wing, fascist, Freemasonic figures in all of Europe. This is actually true, because the man who was the Grand Master of this Masonic order (P-2), Licio Gelli, was invited by Ronald Reagan's Presidential campaign to appear at his inauguration. There are pictures of Ronald Reagan with Licio Gelli. Gelli supported the fascist Mussolini in World War II, then was forced to flee to Argentina, where he supported dictator Juan Peron. Gelli finally returned to Italy in the 1960s and that is when he joined the Grande Oriente, as it was known in Italy, meaning the Masonic Order of Freemasonry. With the support of the Grande Oriente, Gelli was cleared for the his war crimes that he'd been charged with. Gelli, as Grand Master of P-2, made it the most violent and powerful secret political organization in Italy. A former U.S. intelligence officer who became involved with the group called P-2 "a state within a state." Much like the Vatican. There are clearly "political ties" between these organizations and world governments – as evidenced by Gelli and Reagan. We don't normally see them on the surface. Europe is a very small world and so is America. There are many important connections between Europe and America, but they are often hidden, below the surface. I know. I grew up listening to it among private family members.

Let me explain something that you might find quite interesting. We're hearing a lot about this New World Order that former President George Bush originally kept talking about. Europe was the "Old World" and America, of course, after it was discovered, was known as the "New World." In the "Old World," Europe was dominated by the Vatican. The Vatican dominated Europe and Europe dominated the world. It was said that the power behind the Vatican was an order of Freemasonry and believe me, the more one looks into it, the more truth to this fact emerges. It was an occult order of Freemasonry operating from behind the scenes, and thereby exercising influence over European politics. Now, that was an old order, like the

Masonic Order, or an order of priesthood. It was commonly known as a fraternal order. This group, this very small group of people actually "ran the show." Yes, from behind the scenes, with the Vatican out in front as the front organization. The Vatican representing religion would be untouchable. And, of course you wouldn't want to do anything to harm or interfere with God's will.

The power behind the Vatican throne for the past fifteen or sixteen hundred years has been referred to in circles as the "Old World Order." It was the "Order" of the "Old World." Then, when the United States was discovered – we've become know as the "New World." And, therefore there are now religio-political fraternal orders which dominate our country. And through us, dominate the world. And, that is a "New World Order." So, when we hear the word "order," they are talking about a fraternal order, like an order of priesthood, or a Masonic Order. This "New World Order" is operating out of our country.

What you have to remember too, when you say religio-political movement, there has never been a religious movement, throughout the world, that didn't have a little politics involved in it. There has never been a political movement that wasn't a little bit religious. As a matter of fact, at one time in the ancient world, government was religion. And religion was government. Today, in our modern world we are not really aware of that. We naively think that things have always been the way they are in the United States. But, this is not so. There is a profound connection between religion and politics, even in our country. We ostensibly say that we on the outside of these powerful organizations, believe that there is a separation of church and state. The American armed forces hire Chaplains. They become officers in the military. Therefore, they are paid religious leaders to represent God for the government. You have to remember that when you get married, you don't go before God for your marriage. You go before the State and you get a license, before you can talk to God about marriage. And, if your marriage doesn't work out, you don't go to God and talk to him about it, you go to the courts, because that's where the real power is contained.

To draw the point out again, that there is a connection between church and state, just think about the church arena. Inside of the church is just like inside a courtroom.

Symbols are like letters of an alphabet. You put them together and they spell a word, and you put enough of them together and you've got the story. Today, we have the symbol of ARCO, which is the Masonic square, which goes back to Jason and the ARCO-naughts (argonauts). These symbols are images that we may not know the full story about. But, look at these emblems in the oil companies, on cigarette packages, and on food items, and automobile emblems; they are all classic examples.

It has been said that the emblems and symbols dwell deep within the collective unconscious. So, this is not just a coincidence that they happen to be religious, and they also happen to be political. They are also used in advertising campaigns. Everybody is using the same symbols. There are only a finite number of symbols that make any sense, so everybody is going to use them.

Governmental politics is actually a business, a business that has been around a very long time. America is big business, originally founded as a business corporation. The original thirteen colonies were not called colonies. They were called companies. That's why in corporate law every corporation must have a president and a vice president. And, we have a president and a vice president of our corporation – our country. This county, the United States of America is a business. Or, at least it was, as even the U.S. business can show a loss, or whatever. So, there is much chicanery going on both in politics and religion. When you have a financial loss, just remember that there is just so much money out there – out in the world. And, if somebody is losing it, that means it is going somewhere. Therefore, someone is

The biblical Ark of the Covenant has its origins in the ancient Egyptian "Ark of the Law."

making it. When you see a big stock market crash and everyone loses their money, then somebody else just made a lot of money. Really all that amounts to is that this huge amount of money just changed hands. That is what is happening today. Our country is in bad economic straits because somebody is hoarding all the money.

I have an opinion as to who hoards all the money, but I am not going to express it here. I don't feel I have to do that. I think we all understand the Golden Rule, "He who has all the gold makes the rules." There is no real power among the people of this country. There never has been. We understand that the political setup in this country is identical to many in the ancient world. Just know that the movie being enacted on the screen of the world is not actually what is going on, but that there are people behind the screen – behind the scenes, that are actually manipulating the play or movie that most people do not know anything about.

Let's take some of the major religions and find out what is really going on. Even our motion pictures reflect an occult story, they are telling this story. For example, the ancient magical priests of the Celtics had magic wands. And, the magic wands were used to dupe people or to work their magic on them. Magic wands were always made out of holly wood. Consequently, our masters still use Hollywood to manipulate our thinking and to tell us stories. There is a tremendous amount of symbolism in our motion pictures today.

There was such a thing as the "Ark of the Law." It was a box with two handles on it; it had the two winged angels on it, just as we see today in pictures of the Ark of the Covenant of the ancient Hebrews. But thousands of years before the Hebrew nation ever existed we have the "Ark of the Law" of ancient Egypt. That ark was symbolic for a very powerful force that Egypt was able to dominate the world with. With the coming of Western man, the concepts and ideas coming out of Egypt were adopted.

The same magic is being used today, such as in Washington, DC. We see the obelisk, right there in Washington, and it has a very profound meaning that dates

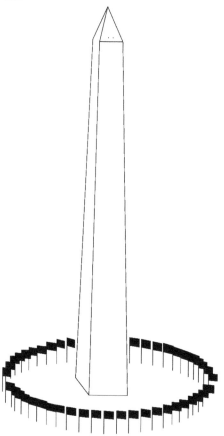

The Washington Monument, yet another ancient Egyptian phallic symbol. In this case the phallic is ringed with the "sacred circle," representing the female reproductive power.

back to ancient Egypt. And on the back of a one dollar bill we see a pyramid with an all seeing eye. Pyramids are found in Egypt. Among esoteric circles throughout the world today, America is referred to as the new Egypt. The coming of the new Egypt. All of American's political, religious, and philosophical systems originated in Egypt. Most people are not aware of that fact. There are some very important things going on that we have just not been kept informed about.

Let me first say, that I am in no way finding fault with – or knocking Christianity. I am saying though, that the religious philosophy that we refer to as Christianity was in fact, at one time already in existence. The basic theme of Christianity was already in existence in all the ancient empires – especially Egypt. It is interesting to know that a man hanging on a cross was never pictured in the first four hundred years of Christianity. They never had a symbol, or an emblem, or a picture anywhere in Christianity of a man hanging on a cross. It was always pictured as a lamb – or a sheep carrying a cross. It was not until the sixth century at one of the great ecumenical councils that it was decided that we should have a man hanging on the cross. That's where the concept of a man hanging on a cross was begun.

There was a man named Jesus. This is historical fact – there was a man named Jesus. His correct name in Hebrew was Jehoshua Ben-Pandira, or Joshua, son of the panther. He lived approximately one hundred years before the Jesus of the Bible would have lived. This man was a teacher of the Essene religion. He was a great teacher. He was a healer, etc. But, a religion grew up in the Roman Empire that we have come to know today as Christianity. I am saying that Christianity is, in fact, another expression of a far more ancient religious philosophy that has all of the earmarks of being one more retelling of the story. That's why the Bible is referred to as the Greatest Story Ever Told. Even the Babylonians had their holy man come down from the holy mountain with their tablets of stone. They had their Messiah that died on the cross and who died on the upright tree and who was buried and who was born again after three days., etc.

This doesn't lessen or in any way take away from the story. No. Not in any way. This is not saying that Jesus was not the Christ. What I am saying, though, is that the story may not necessarily be exactly what we think it is. There is a history to religion that we are not often treated to, especially in America. We are fond of saying that we have the freedom to think and have freedom of speech, etc. That's true. We do have freedom of speech – up to a certain point. But there are certain things that are not accepted socially, that we just don't talk about. In my family, many years ago, we just didn't talk about religion and politics. Politics and religion were

The Washington Monument in the District of Columbia. The capstone of an obelisk is known as a pyramidion.

off base and we simply weren't supposed to talk about them. Now that I am much older, I understand why. Because religion and politics are very volatile subjects, and a lot of political and religious leaders do not want you to talk about politics and religion. All of this material being covered has been hotly debated. It's been debated to the point where most people say, "Look, I don't care."

What's wrong with that? Because the more people talk about something the more they investigate it, the more a subject is discussed, the more it causes other information comes out. I'm saying it's about time that we do discuss religion and politics. I think there is a very important connection between the two, and its about time we look at that connection. I see nothing wrong with the teachings of Christianity.

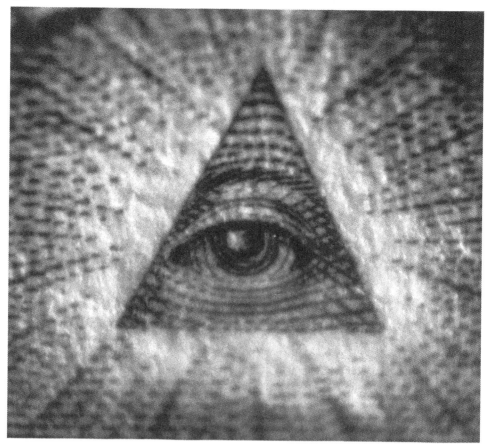

The all-seeing eye of the Illumninati, as seen on the back of the U.S. dollar bill.

In fact, I myself adhere and believe the teachings to be a very fine and fundamental concept, concerning the way to lead one's life. But you must understand that it is a story that has been retold and retold and retold. So, if you understand it correctly – what I would call understanding Christianity – you would understand the basic principles that are being discussed, rather than hanging everything on just a story. Reason and logic alone would tell you that you have to ask questions. Did all those people back in biblical times go around with tape recorders or court stenographers, and check every single word every prophet spoke, or check up on every character in the Bible. . . what he did, where he went, and what he spoke? Did they have tape recorders?

How do we know that every single word must be exactly that word? And, every single event must coincide with every single word? There's only one way you could get a book to coincide and fall in line completely as a beautiful whole story, as if it was written as a story. So, that is what I'm saying, the Bible was written as a very beautiful story if you understand that that's all it was, a story.

Now, there's some good history in the Bible. I am not saying that the Bible is not the word of God. I just don't believe that it is the only Divine book written in the world.

If you understand that the world was, at one time, dominated by the Vatican and there was a World War – in fact, there have been two World Wars between powerful secret societies for power on this Earth. One is the New World Order as opposed to the old world order. I believe that is why the World Wars have been fought. That's why we're having skirmishes all over the world.

> *We are not going to achieve a new world order without paying for it in blood as well as in words and money.*
> —Arthur Schlesinger, Jr., in Foreign Affairs (July/August 1995)

I have two books in my collection right now, one was printed in 1969, another in 1972, or 1973...talking about how Yugoslavia was going to be divided between the secret societies. They were going to go in and cause a lot of confusion and chaos and break up the status quo there purposely, in relation to this New World Order coming. So, there's got to be some connections here between what's happening today when there are very knowledgeable people that have foretold that these things were going to happen in Yugoslavia. Nothing happens by happenstance, but this is all being orchestrated by some small group of people. I truly don't think that there are a lot of things that happen by chance – I don't think the important things politically are allowed to happen by chance. Keep in mind when you hear government officials talk about crime and drugs, saying they can't seem to get a handle on the drug traffic and they can't seem to get a handle on the crime in the streets and they're just not able to get a handle on these serious problems. Just remember that almost sixty years ago the United States got a handle on Nazi Germany. They did get control of the standing army of Adolph Hitler on the other side of the world.

My point is that any crime that goes on or any drug trafficking that goes on, it is going on with the knowledge and consent – if not cooperation – of a very powerful group of people who have their reasons. It might just be to keep you frightened to death and keep you worried about the future so that you will accept anything that they give you – any kind of idea they will come up with to distract you from the real truth. They have the power to shut down anything they want anytime they please. So if something is going on, it is going on with their help, or they're allowing it to happen politically. This is the same thing that happened in Nazi Germany. Adolph Hitler told the German people that in order to keep the crime off the streets, and avoid all the trouble that was going on, the confusion, that all they would have to do is elect him.

Let me just say that I don't believe that the whole world is totally controlled. But reason and logic alone dictate the possibility of that happening. Always, anytime a country goes to war or is building up for a future war, all countries picture their coming enemy as a desperate murderer, killing babies or whatever. You've got to generate that kind of furor (Fuhrer!) in the people's minds so that it will justify going to war with this terrible person – or a whole body of people in any given country – like Saddam Hussein.

These hidden agendas are contrived by the media and the press. They led America, if not instigated the energy, into war with Saddam. This could be called outright propaganda. Although, it really is NEWS! It is called the evening news. Of course, we see these terrible evil people (on the news). Then, later on we'll hear that the President has made some kind of an arrangement with that person and give him fifty billion dollars of our money and then you see them patting each other on the back, to go off to their local Masonic lodges together. But come to find out, this is a business arrangement. Yesterday, this guy was our duplicable enemy and today he is our friend and we are supporting his agenda. We are being duped. Throughout the history of humankind the vast majority of people have been duped by a few that are in power. We sit here like sitting suckers, with a sign hung out on our front American lawns, saying, "Come on, here is your next ready made sucker!" Today, the American public – the plain old ordinary American public, has been duped from day one. And, we continue to allow this horrendous duplicity.

A few years ago a movie came out that was called *Network*. In it, the network broadcaster said that the general view of the people was, "Just leave me alone. I don't care about all of this. Just let me have my radial tires, my beer, my remote control and television, and I'll be numbed-out happy." Everyday the powers of government keep moving on you – little by little, until one day there is no more freedom. And that is exactly what is happening in our country today. In my opinion we have already lost most of our real freedom to the federal government. What is it that might be coming? Henry Kissinger said it best.

> *Today, America would be outraged if U.N. troops entered Los Angeles to restore order* [referring to the 1991 LA Riot]. *Tomorrow they will be grateful! This is especially true if they were told that there were an outside threat from beyond* [i.e., an "extraterrestrial" invasion], *whether real or promulgated, that threatened our very existence. It is then that all peoples of the world will plead to deliver them from this evil. The one thing every man fears is the unknown. When presented with this scenario, individual rights will be willingly relinquished for the guarantee of their well-being granted to them by the World Government.*

—Dr. Henry Kissinger,
Bilderberger Conference, Evians, France, 1991

I believe that real freedom is in the mind. In the intellectual brain. That's where real freedom is happening. And there is something to do with our spirituality in the mind which brings freedom. That is the one place that the government fears most, you mind, your thinking. You ability to be yourself and do your own thinking, call your own shots, and be your own person.

That's exactly what governments do not want for every world citizen. They try to keep you busy so that you can pay your bills, pay your taxes, take care of your house, and when you finish taking care of all the details of survival, the government hopes you will not have the time, or will try not to think about some of the things that we have been talking about in this book. And, if there is leisure time among much of the population, they will give you entertainment, to keep you completely distracted – anything to prevent you from thinking more deeply. Just make sure there is plenty of drugs, plenty of entertainment, a little sex, drugs and rock and roll, and that will keep the people happy – keep them occupied so they will stay out of the way – controlled!

I am not saying that people should not be able to do this. But, it would behoove you to get an education, read, study, investigate what I am saying on your own. Take the responsibility to find these things out that I am reporting here. Go to the library, check out and read something about the occult world, about how we are manipulated, especially in our politics and religion. I could provide you with a list of literally hundreds of very informative and interesting volumes on these subjects.

Today, there are many secret fraternal organization that are interconnected. They have a death grip on world power, behind the scenes. Our world and lives are so full of symbolism. For example, once again, on the back of the American dollar bill, the great seal of America. It is filled with occult meaning. You will find on the dollar bill, the eagle, which comes from the ancient concept of the Phoenix, and has thirteen stars above it. The thirteen stars are arranged in the configuration of the Star of David, or the hexagram. Most people think the thirteen stars represent the original thirteen colonies. In the first place, why did they have to have thirteen colonies? Why couldn't they have twenty-seven, or four, or ten? When one understands that the number thirteen is a very important, profound Masonic number, and that many of the founding fathers of this country were Freemasons, as well as Rosicrucians, then you will follow this connecting thread of material to see what was actually being created. They knew what they were doing when they divided this country into thirteen colonies. The number thirteen is not an unlucky number for them. It is an unlucky number for you.

The number thirteen comes from Jesus and his twelve apostles. The twelve apostles were the cornerstones of the new era, and Jesus is referred to as the "Chief Cornerstone that the builders rejected." Twice in the New Testament Jesus is referred to as the Chief Cornerstone. *Chief Cornerstone* is a Greek word that means "the peak of a pyramid." That's why there is a little pyramid on top of a big pyramid on the left-hand side on the back of a dollar bill. That is a Chief Cornerstone. It is symbolic of Jesus. The pyramid also has thirteen layers. As a matter of fact, thirteen is all over the back of the American one dollar bill. I would have to say that the Illuminati, under their various guises and names, run the affairs of the world.

Freemasonry is a very ancient fraternal order. For thousands of years it was made up of many different groups which loosely fit into an association of builders, going back to the most ancient times in which men built with bricks – such as the pyramids of Egypt, and all the ancient temples. They were brick builders. Even today we refer to one working with bricks as a brick mason. The trade of a mason, or the conceptual idea of building with bricks, was a building trade. There were men who did nothing but that, and they were referred to as brick masons. They came down through ancient history and began to jealously guard each other's work, and not let any newcomers come into the trade. They had "unions," so to speak. We do the same thing today. Later on in 1717 many occult orders and many of the building trade orders of Freemasonry came together in London and began what we call Freemasonry, on the modern-day scale. Modern-day Freemasonry was started in 1717, but the idea goes back to ancient Egypt and other ancient civilizations.

If you understand that the ancient masons built their world with brick, then you understand why today's Freemasons say of themselves that they are the modern-day builders of the world. They not only build the building that you live in and do business in, they are building the *structure* of the world, as Freemasons. They are building your religions, your political establishments – all you have to do is go to the library and get reference books on flags, national coats of arms, symbols and emblems of different countries, and different international organizations. They are all Freemasonic symbols. Also interesting is the fact that a lot of the graffiti that is being seen in large cities throughout this country are Masonic symbols. Only high degree Freemasons would know that. A lot of the black gangs and the Mexican gangs spread graffiti around our cities. Much of that graffiti is very powerful Masonic symbolism. This leads me to wonder how these kids know those symbols. I am suggesting that there is some connection between occult Freemasonry and the spread of violence and crime in our country. I think we had better look at some very uncomfortable, but very positively important connections that can be made between crime on the streets, and the elitist people that run this country – who are allowing it to happen. There's a reason. I think that crime in this country is being allowed for a purpose. A lot of people may feel this way, but nobody is saying it publicly.

Now, we must ask, where is this going? Where are the occult orders that control most of the important political and religious events of this world trying to lead this planet? I think that for hundreds of years there has been a concerted effort to lead the world into a New World Order – a completely new civilization where human beings will no longer be the same type of humans that they were in the past. We are being guided into a new age. There is a New World Order that is being orchestrated. All the violence and destruction that we are seeing today is destroying the old order in preparation for a new order. You cannot construct a high rise building where there is an old shack, until you tear down the old shack.

Today, we are having wars and bloodshed everywhere so that we can destroy the power base of "the good ol' boys" in different countries, then a "New World

Order" can be set up. I cannot escape the conclusion that there is someone very, very high up and extremely wise and perceptive as to how to make things happen to bring about a certain conclusion. I tend to believe that that being or entity is something spiritual. I believe there is something spiritual happening in our world today. But it also uses men – powerful people. And these powerful men often get greedy, and may not follow their "higher calling" properly. They are only human, and power is intoxicating. I am concerned for the future because of the loss of individuality and the loss of the human ability, freedom and the liberty to think. That is one thing about this country I am thankful for – that we have the opportunity to discuss things intelligently with each other and give each other the opportunity to be heard because that is how we grow. However, I think that personal evolution is being stifled.

More and more the governmental powers from behind the scenes are quietly making sure that people don't talk too much about things that are controversial. I think that human minds are being remolded, and reprogrammed so that people don't really have to think a whole lot anymore. We just go along to get along and whatever the government says, we do, whatever the church says, we do, and whatever our assigned authorities say to do, we do. I think that that is where the real problem is going to exist.

Let's step back a moment and consider the Vatican as it existed in the time of A.D. 600's. The Earth was regarded as being the center of the Universe. People were controlled by the Church. They lived for the Church. The only hope they had was that they would go to heaven, and not to hell. And everything else was basically business as usual. That worked quite well for hundreds of years. But this system became rather difficult to uphold when people found out that the Earth wasn't the center of the Universe. Then the Church began to lose a lot of its credibility and power. Now, I think a few people are trying to gain similar power and control over people, but not necessarily through the Church. They are trying to regain such power through new secular means because the people have been infected with this idea of freedom and liberty and individual rights to think for themselves. Consequently, the Church is not going to operate well. Churches never operate well in an environment where people are allowed to be themselves and do their own thinking and call their own shots in their lives. So now, instead of being afraid of going to hell, people are being conditioned to be afraid of total destruction through world wars, or environmental collapse, or some other terrible catastrophe coming, even an alien invasion. There is enough out there that some very brilliant people can come up with something that will scare the life out of all of us.

Not to mention that nature itself can be very frightening with such phenomena as volcanoes, earthquakes, etc. And, I wonder how much of that is man-made. There is a considerable high technology in this world that is operational, too. The underlying agenda has been control, and more control through fear. So one of the basic messages I am trying to get across is to rid yourself of fear. Rid yourself of fear and educate yourself. Become informed as broadly as you possibly can. Go to the library and check out books on the occult history of this world.

A word of warning. The word occult has been grossly misrepresented by the media. Most people, when they hear the word occult, think immediately of demons and the boogey man. This is yet another way we are being manipulated because we are being told, over and over again, that there is something mysterious and dark and unnerving, and something very fearful about the occult. Everything else is okay, we are told. Religion is fine. But the occult offers something that is very dangerous. Once you understand what is going on, you find out that some very crafty people have not told you what they are doing and how they are doing it, and they are working some real heavy duty magic upon you. You are nothing more than a sitting duck, because you don't understand the process.

The word occult means hidden. That, simply, is all it means. Anything that is hidden is occult. I'm talking about the hidden powers behind the throne; the hidden powers behind religion; the hidden innuendoes behind everyday symbolism. People who have accepted the authorities as the truth find it very difficult to accept the truth as authority. Authority does not always come with the truth. And, truth does not always come with authority. The bottom line is, no matter what you believe, there is a truth that resonates with your heart and everyone elses. There is a factual truth that can be pointed out, but you have to look for it. If, however, you go along to get along; if you accept your government's view of everything, and if you accept your particular religious persuasion of things, then you are no different than the Hindus, the Buddhists, the Muslims and all the other people we condemn throughout the world – or those silly radicals who follow the views of their leaders and blow up buildings without asking questions. We may, like them, find ourselves being in wars and killing people without even questioning this authority, because they are doing it for the Lord. In what way are we any different if we do the same? What is important is that you maintain your own individuality as an intelligent human being, and do your own homework so your thinking becomes grounded in the truth.

In this particular time in which we are living, to be able to speak freely, is going to be very important in the very near future. Our freedoms are being very closely watched, and are being monitored. There is the possibility that we are going to lose our freedom of speech quite soon. On this planet there are no passengers, we're all crew, so we all have a stake in what is happening in this world. Whether we want to deal with it or not, we have to face what is going on in the world around us, and especially with our rights as free citizens.

H. G. Wells said that, "Civilization is nothing more than a race between education and catastrophe." And, that is what we have coming. Catastrophe is looking at us from all corners of the globe. Certainly, from the standpoint of the New World Order. The Talmud states that, "If there is no knowledge, then there is no understanding." If there is no understanding, then there is no knowledge, and that's what we have today. A whole lot of no understanding. It is about time for people who *do know*, to speak up.

President Woodrow Wilson once said, "If you want to make enemies, just try to change something." So, I know that anyone who tries to bring to the public the facts behind the world that we live in, is going to be criticized and condemned. I believe that there are enough people in this world who want to know the truth and who want to be willing to stand and fight for it. Not in the violent, literal sense, but with higher moral values, upholding free ethical standards, and a deeper understanding to be well-informed.

Let me explain one of the main problems and tragedies in the world today. In the case of one who knows, or has wisdom, he is usually aware that he doesn't know everything. It is usually the man who thinks he knows everything, who doesn't know anything. One of the most important ways of learning anything today in our society is through symbols and emblems. Emblems are like words. If you can't read the emblems or symbols, you don't know what the story is revealing. This is especially true in religion. We are seeing so much in what is said to be religion, and, in fact, it is nothing more than politics. And, of course, politics are religion, and religion is politics. There has never been a religious movement on Earth that wasn't a little political. And, there has never been a political movement that didn't have a little religion involved in it.

I want to focus on the religion that is prominent in our country, and that is Christianity. Before I get into this subject, I want to emphasize that I don't appreciate anyone placing anyone else into a narrow box, or pigeon-holing me and deciding who I am in my belief systems, or where I am coming from. Because, if you don't know me, you don't know where I am coming from. I am not a Communist, I am not a Nazi, I am not a racist, I am just a human being with something to say. I belong to no political party, consequently, I am not coming from any particular place. I am just a human being, a researcher, a teacher, and an investigative writer. I enjoy doing what I do, and have been centered for over thirty-five years doing what I do, and it's about time I bring my work to the public.

Now we see in this country, on television, a lot about Christianity. We see Presidents, and Congressmen, and Senators, and everybody – all the Civic leaders are all into Christianity and going to church and being fine people. However, for being fine people, we find that many are not really fine. As a matter of fact, an honest politician, these days, is one who did not take a bribe that he didn't earn. So, let's face it, our system of government has fallen apart. It is collapsing all around us, and the reason why is that it is built on lies. Perhaps one of the greatest lies, or misconceptions, and let's be generous here to maybe identify some misunderstandings, is the truth about Christianity. I would like to deal with Christianity first and get that out of the way, because until such time as the people understand where Christianity came from, how it was organized, and why it teaches what it does, you're not going to understand the mentality behind it. And, we are talking about a white mentality.

If we go back, say ten to fifteen thousand years ago into the ancient world, you should understand that they didn't have the modern-day conveniences that we do. They didn't have the television to occupy their time and waste their lives. They didn't have the nice warm homes and cars and all such things to keep them occupied. Those were very hostile times in an inhospitable world. It was fearful and cold, and very difficult for human beings to survive. Most especially in Europe. Most adults died from around twenty-five to thirty years of age. It was a very hostile world for humans to live, to eke out the barest of existence.

We are talking, again, about ten to fifteen thousand year ago. It was obvious from the beginning, according to the best material that has been provided to us from history, and that's the best we have from the ancient records, that the first enemy for man, was darkness. The first thing man realized that was frightening to his world, was just plain darkness. It was bad enough to live through the daytime, but when the sun went down it got scary, because there were predator animals out there, there were enemies lurking in the bush. So nighttime became very fearful to our first hominids. When you understand that kind of a world, and those conditions, from there you begin to appreciate how they perceived the coming of that orb of day, or the Sun, as something to look forward to with relief. Because when the Sun went down, you got nothing to look forward to but potentially frightful problems. And, of course, if you have ever been out on a cold night, you can imagine what our first ancestors fifteen thousand years ago had to look forward to when it got real cold at night. You can then appreciate why they would look forward to the coming of the Sun, or the coming of that great orb of day.

Now, if you begin to see how these philosophies would come into people's minds and begin to grow, and their children growing up would begin to accept the same philosophies and ideas and promote them to their children, and their children to their children, you begin to see how the philosophy became one of "war" between light and darkness. That which was light was good, of course, because the light was usually peaceful, and it was good, and that which was dark was bad.

Thereby, this primitive understanding was the basis for this animosity between the light and darkness. Well, we know we have seen a lot of that, because that is carried over into our society sociologically, regarding the war between light and darkness. As I said, light was good, and dark was bad. The Sun, of course, was the light of the world, and they understood that. The ancients were not stupid. They saw that the Sun was not God. They never believed that the Sun was God, but they believed that it was the reproduction of God, it was the offspring of God, it was the closest symbol that they could grasp to represent deity in heaven. So they figured that since your son looks a lot like you, well maybe God looks a lot like the Sun, or that the Sun looks a lot like the Father. So they realized this about the Sun, and I am using the word as an Anglo-Saxon word today. The orb in the sky, or whatever you want to call it, back then was understood to be the descendant of the Father, who was the Creator of the Heavens. So, therefore, they realized that this Sun did not belong to anyone, it belonged to the heavens, or it belonged to God, so it was God's Son. Every morning it was in the sky, or it was in heaven, so, therefore, God's Son was in heaven. As I said, it was the Son, or the offspring of the Father. They believed that no one has ever seen the Father. No one can see God, but if the Sun looks like God, then maybe the Sun/Son mimicked God. So, when you have seen the Sun/Son, then maybe you have seen the Father.

Now, incidentally, it is interesting as to why the ancients believed that God was a father, because in the most ancient world they associated the creation of the humans, the creation on the Earth, with the Mother. It was only until the coming of the early Roman Empire that the emphasis was put on the male. As contrasted to the African, which is based on the female principle. And even the Greeks borrowed many things from Africa, with one example being the Feast of Sophia, which was based on feminine wisdom. And, as I said, the ancient people knew that no one had ever seen God, no one can see God, but if you have seen the Sun/Son, you have seen the Father. The reason why the ancients believed this postulate, as some of the ancient people believed that God was a father, was because of rain. Rain was perceived to be the fluid from the Father that gives a life, or brings life to Mother Earth. So, when Mother Earth is impregnated with the fluid from the Father in Heaven, then the Mother gives birth to all life. So that is where the concept of God the Father comes from, from rain.

The area that we call today, Israel, was in very ancient times called Cana. The people there called Canaanites, and they celebrated the great marriage feast, so to speak, between God, the Father, and Mother Earth, and all of the light that the two of them produced for us. This very ancient celebration was in the Spring, and was called The Marriage Feast of Cana. This was where God's Son was symbolically asked by Mother Earth to draw water to make it rain, so that the grapes could grow and we could have a wine feast, which was called The Marriage Feast of Cana. That's where that comes from.

Of course, the sun gives life to us, and gives us our energy. It gives energy to all living things. Then, we eat those living things to give us energy, so the sun is giving up its energy for us to live. Just as the ancients believed that God's Son gave His life, so that we may live. The Sun/Son, of course, represented this, which is interesting, because the ancient Egyptians said that as long as the sun comes up in the morning, there is going to be life. There is obviously going to be life forever, as long as the sun comes up! Therefore, the sun gives everlasting life on the Earth – but not for you, only on the Earth is there everlasting life. Of course, God's Son is our Savior, in that He is risen. Moreover, the ancients said that the sun, as wonderful as it was, was not going to save anybody if it did not come up in the morning. If it doesn't come up in the morning, we are dead. He is our Salvation, He is our Savior, *only* if He has risen. And the Egyptians called that risen sun in the morning, Horus. Horus was God's son, that was the name they came up for him in Egypt. Horus. And, they said that in the morning all Egyptians would get up to see the Sun come up, like an Easter sunrise service, and they would see the Son/Sun come up as He was rising. You would go out to see Horus, and He is risen. That's why even today the sun comes up on the Horus-risen – or the horizon.

You had better thank the Father for sending His Sun/Son, because He is your life, and He is your salvation. Ancients breathed a sigh of relief when they saw the sun come up, because they became more secure in their world. When they saw the sun come up everything became clear, and they could see all the animals, and they weren't afraid of the dark anymore. So, consequently, the Sun/Son took on the position of the Prince of Peace, because everyone felt much better when the sun came up. So, He was then considered the Prince of Peace.

Now, as we've said, the sun in Egypt was called Horus when it rose in the morning. And that is where he had twelve segments of his lifespan – in the daytime. Half of 24 hours, or 12 hours of light. That's where we get the word hours, hours come from Horus. Hours, or Horus. So therefore, the sun would come up on the horizon. It is interesting, too, in the Egyptian way of thinking, that there was a second Sun/Son. God had a second son, who was equal to the first, but was bad. If you are familiar with Egyptian mythology, you would know that his name was Set, and, of course, Set was the evil son. He was dark, so that made him evil, and he would only come out as the Prince of Darkness after dark – at sun-set. So, of course it got dark after the sun went down, so Set came out when it got dark and became the boogey-man who was going to get you, since he was dark. Therefore, that made him bad.

Now you have the two brothers, Horus and Set, one was light and one was darkness. The original trinity in Egypt was the three lifespans of the sun, or the three lifespans in life. Morning, noon, and night. With people we have the newborn, the mature, and the dying. This is where we got the original concept for the trinity. In Egypt, Horus was the beginning, the sun coming up on the horizon, which was the newborn. Then, at twelve noon, the sun was high over the pyramid. There was no shadow on the pyramid, so they knew it was twelve, therefore, he was called at that point the "most high," as you couldn't go any higher in the sky. So Horus was called the most high. Therefore you have in the morning God's Sun/Son, Horus, and then the "most high" at twelve noon, and then at night you have Set. From there you have your original trinity.

The religion has taken all sorts of twists and turns coming down through history, but this is the basis for what we call today, Christianity. If you don't understand that, then you don't appreciate where the stories originate from. It has always amazed me how many people will understand Christianity, but not understand that Christianity is nothing more than a retelling of the same age-old stories that have come down through time. As a matter of fact, the Bible is not called the greatest collection of *facts* ever assembled. No, it is called "the greatest *story* ever told."

This window, called a sun window, is one of the oldest sun symbols from the ancient world.

The reason why it is the greatest *story* ever told is because if you do a little homework, you're going to find out it is the oldest story ever told. As a matter of fact, it is the *only* story ever told. It is called astro-theology, the study and the worship of the heavens.

If you go out in the night time and look into the sky, what are you looking at? You are looking at the sky. What is another name for the sky. Another word for sky, is heaven. Well, that is where the sun is at. At twelve noon the sun is high in heaven, so, therefore, they said that God's Sun/Son was in heaven. Of course, they never believed that when

The sun's cycle was divided into 12 houses (hours/ months) giving us the Constellations of the Zodiac.

they died they would go to heaven with God's sun. At least, they knew that much. At twelve noon the sun was the most high, consequently they said that God's Son was twelve when he was in God's temple. God's temple was, of course, the heavens, and at twelve noon he is in the temple. That is why he was twelve when he was in the temple.

Everlasting life came from God's sun. And the sun was round. It was a circle in the sky. So the ancients saw life as a round circle, "the circle of life," which was pictured or represented by the sun. The way they kept time, then, was on a round calendar. Today we call them sundials. That's where they came from, the round calendars. As a matter of fact, the Aztecs, and the Mayans, and the ancient Mexicans kept the round sun calendars. Now the sun calendars that were in Egypt were round and were divided into twelve parts, just as all sun calendars are today, twelve parts, displaying not only twelve hours, but twelve months. Each one of the months was called a helper to the sun, because it helped the sun do his job on Earth in that particular month.

Later on, those particular months were called houses, because in the Babylonian scheme of things they began to develop what was called astrology. So each one of the months became a house. Therefore, the Sun, God's Son, the light of the world, who is our salvation, because he has risen, had twelve helpers, or twelve apostles. And the sun also enters into each one of those houses of the zodiac, or each one of those constellations of the zodiac, at the thirtieth degree, and it leaves at the thirty-third degree. Therefore, they said that the Sun/Son begins His ministry at thirty and dies at thirty-three. This is very, very old knowledge, as a matter of fact, there are many books that trace at least fifteen other major religions that have used God's Son as the "light of the world" in the same context, in the same religious philosophy that was developed for the worship of God's sun. Yes, there were at least fifteen other major religions, ancient religions, that used the story. One of the reference books that documents this, right off the top of my head, is *The World's Sixteen Crucified Saviors*, by Kersey Graves. This is a great book for that kind of a study and is available through The Book Tree.

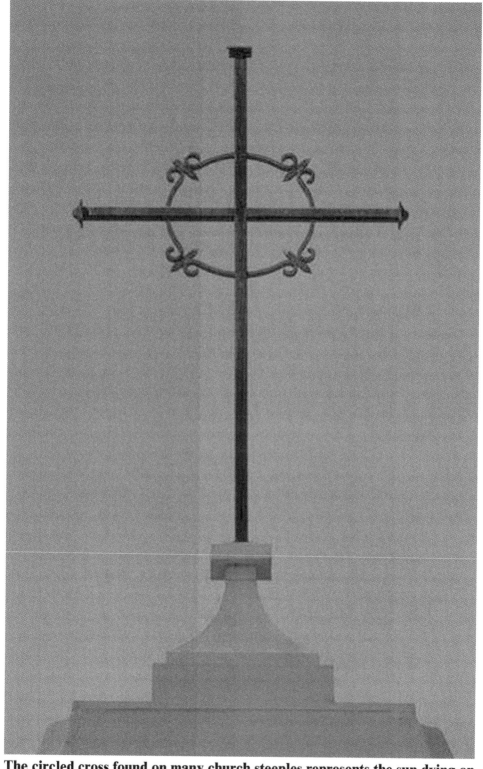

The circled cross found on many church steeples represents the sun dying on the cross of the zodiac. The cycle of four seasons is also displayed.

The sun on the cross associated with bell symbolism within a sacred archway.

There are so many interesting points that I feel are valuable to bring out in relation to the subject of religion. Christianity has always labeled these ancient religions as being pagan, which gives a negative connotation. The word pagan actually means someone who lives in the country, a mountain dweller, or someone who lives outside of a city. That name was given to someone who lived up in the mountains, because in Rome, after Christianity was adopted, the religion was thought to be sophisticated. There was little sophistication to be found outside of the cities. Once Caesar became a Christian then everybody could be a Christian, so therefore, it became the State religion. So it was in high style to be a Christian. Consequently, you were considered very intelligent if you became a Christian at that time, you were very in, you were modern if you were a Christian in Rome. Once it was accepted fully, and then it became the thing to be. Of course, the people out in the hills, the farmers, the poor people out in the country, on the outside of Rome that have lived the same way for ten thousand years, well, those were pagans. They didn't understand a new "take" on things. So it became a disparaging remark about poor people of the soil, people who were farmers, people who didn't know all of this high-fangled, new religious thing that Rome had come up with as a new belief

The cross with the circle of the sun is a very common symbol, in both ancient and modern times.

system. They were just people, and the working class people were called pagans. That is where the word came from in ancient times. Anybody who wasn't with the "in" crowd in Rome, with the new religion, was considered a pagan.

Now, let us get back to the sundial. The sundial was round because the sun was round. It kept track of the months because it was divided into twelve equal parts. While this might be dry religious philosophy being discussed, it has a motive at the end, so I caution you to not disregard this discussion too quickly, because it is going to get interesting very soon. The connection with the rest of this material will be revealed.

Now, as we have said, the calendar was divided into twelve parts, or the twelve helpers of the sun, and that is where we get the twelve apostles of the Son. The ancient peoples came to notice something very interesting, as they were very observant. Unlike us, we are too busy these days to observe anything. The ancient people had time to observe, and they found out something that is interesting during winter, on what we call the Winter Solstice. Up to December 22nd, the Sun had kept moving. Each day the sun kept moving on a little portion of the sundial. You could tell each day that the sun was moving by watching the sundial. As the sun was moving further and further South, bringing on our Winter, they would notice that it would go further and further, until it stopped, and then they said, "Thank God, the thing has stopped, because if it keeps going its going to be gone completely." So, it stopped, and it stopped on December 22nd. Then they noticed that for three days, on December 22nd, 23rd, and 24th, every morning it was still sitting in the same place. It had not moved any further and hadn't returned back the other way any further. So, they figured that anything that didn't move, must be dead. Consequently, they assumed that the sun must be dead. On the 25th, they noticed that the sun had moved the opposite way one degree, so again they assumed that the thing must be alive now. Therefore, December 25th was the Sun/Son's birthday. But before that they said that God's Sun/Son had died, and been dead for three days.

Of course, we have the big celebration of God's Son being born on December 25th, the sun's "birthday." So, now when you take that round calendar, with twelve individual months, or twelve helpers, or apostles, you divide the circle from the Winter Solstice, which is the middle of Winter, right down through the circle and to the bottom, which would be the Summer Solstice. You then draw another straight line from the other side and go across, making a cross, that is when the Spring Equinox, occurs, and into the Autumn Equinox. Now you've got a circle with a cross in it. That is why today almost all churches that you drive by will have the circle in the cross, mounted on the steeple. People normally don't notice, but look next time. It is usually there.

The circle is the sun that dies on the cross of the zodiac. On the ancient calendar, you divide the Winter and the Summer Solstice from the Autumn and Spring Equinox, thereby creating a cross on the circle, and the circle is the Sun/Son dying on the cross.

As we said, the sun was born on December 25th, and every year they said that the sun was "born again." Now, for you to be born again, that means that you have to go under water to be born again. Why? You know of the common Christian religious ritual, that you must be baptized under water to be born again. Where does that come from? That comes from the fact that when you were born the first time, your Mother broke water and you were submerged in water for the first time.

So, if you are going to be born again, you have got to go back under the water again. Nothing holy about it, just plain old life. And, that's the way philosophies came about in the world. People just looked at the world around them, watched the way things worked, and had to get in line with it. They couldn't make the Universe do what they wanted, so they had to get in line with it to form their religious philosophies and ideas from what was there. So, the baptism had to do with the Mother's water, rather than the River Jordan! It had nothing to do with the River Jordan (except in a symbolic way).

Now for more on the sun. Light was always associated with truth and the lie was always the work of darkness. Therefore, the Sun/Son was the light and the truth. And, He brought the truth and the light. As a matter of fact, it is said of the Son that He was the truth and the light. That is why, incidentally, that we have in our jury system today in America twelve jurors (or sun's "helpers"), who helped bring the truth to light.

Also, about Winter time. Winter was always associated with death, because in the Winter everything dies. So Winter was always associated with death, and, of course, the sun dies in Winter. And, this is a very important point. They said of the sun that when it died on December 22nd, that it had "passed over." We use that term today, that when you pass on, when you pass away, you pass over. The sun had passed over to the death of Winter, to the coming new life of Spring. So that in the Spring He came back to life. And also brought life back to the Earth. So He had passed over, He had passed on, or passed away.

The ancient Egyptians had a celebration on the first day of Spring, and they called it the Passover. They celebrated the Passover, because the sun had passed over from the death of Winter, to the new life of Spring. That's where the Passover ritual comes from. On the first day of Spring all of a sudden everything that is dead, now comes alive again. Therefore, God's Sun/Son is bringing everything to life back on the Earth again, as He is the symbol of everlasting life. And, as I previously said, that new life is for the Earth, but not for you. The particular month that He comes back in the Spring with new life was, in the most ancient calendars, in Virgo, the Virgin. Therefore, it was said that God's Son/Son was born of a virgin. That is where that came from in our religious views.

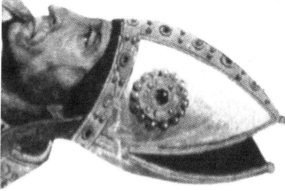

The Papal headdress is really a "fish head," representing the Age of Pisces.

Another view is that God's Sun/Son feeds His followers. One story tells of God's Son feeding His followers with two fishes. Anybody who knows anything about astrology knows that the two fishes is the symbol for the Age of Pisces. The current Age of Pisces, of the two fishes, is a little over two thousand years in length. We are nearing the end of that age right now. If you understand that the twelve apostles were the twelve months of the year, or the twelve hours of light, and the twelve hours of darkness, you can understand that each one of those twelve apostles, or months, was given to a particular astrological constellation. Cancer, Sagittarius, etc.

The old Age of Pisces, or the old age of the fishes, when God's Son feeds his people with the two fishes, is a little over two thousand years old in length. Each one of the constellations is two thousand years in length, in the astrological scheme of things. So, the constellation of Pisces began about two thousand years ago, with the rule of Rome. And Rome was said to have ruled under the Age of Pisces, the two fishes, and that is why we get the idea that God's Son fed the people with the two fishes. The closing of this age also signifies why the "New World Order" is taking power from the "Old World," or Rome, at the end of this Piscean Age.

After the decline of Egypt, Rome came into power and picked up many Egyptian ideas and customs. It's just like everything else, everyone borrows from everybody else, we think we don't, but we do. One person comes out with a smashing movie, and four others then come out with the same general movie. So everyone borrows from everyone else, and that's true of religion. The only problem is understanding who had the original concept. *All of this* began in Egypt. With Egypt we are talking about Africa, and in Africa we are talking about black people.

So we have each one of those ages being about two thousand years long, each one of the constellation ages, and we have God's Sun/Son, the light of the world, coming into the Age of Pisces with the coming of the rule of Rome. That is why the Pope has the fish's hat, the fish's miter. The hat of the Pope is actually the fish of Dagon, or the fish God of the two fishes. Now, we have been in that astrological period of time under which God's Sun/Son has ruled the world in the Age of Pisces for right around two thousand years. And an age, or eon, is a little over two thousand years in length. That means we are just over two thousand years into the Age of Pisces. The next age to come, if you look at any astrological chart, is the Age of Aquarius. Therefore, we are living in "the last days," of the Age of Pisces. When the

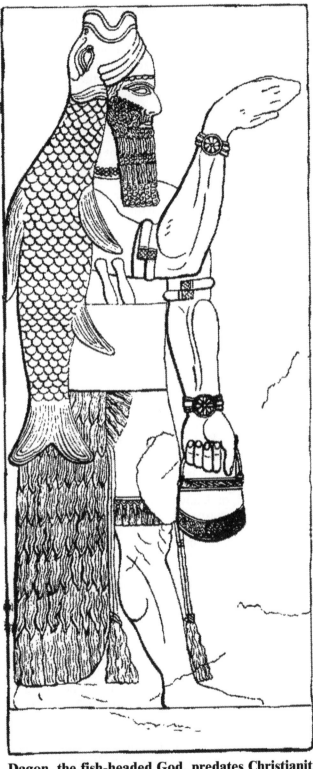

Dagon, the fish-headed God, predates Christianity by thousands of years.

Messiah comes again, he is asked by his disciples in the Book of Luke, 22:10, what he will come back as. He says to go into the town and go into the house of the man with the water pitcher. So here is the Sun/Son, symbolized in Pisces, and the rest of the astrological "signs" (12 "disciples") are asking him what he will do next, when he gets to the end of Age of Pisces. We are now going into the age of the man with the water pitcher. The man with the water pitcher is the symbol for Aquarius. Again, I have to say that the Bible is filled with astrology. It is not known for astrology, and that is what we have to qualify. Once you look at it differently, the symbolism becomes obvious and it is all over the place. The Bible writers knew exactly what they were doing.

Of course, ministers never point this out on Sundays in church. In Christianity they denounce astrology as being evil. Christians say that astrology is evil and bad, from the Devil. Add a "d" to evil, and you have Devil. Take an "o" out of good, and you have God. In the Old Testament, Moses says to God's people to have nothing to do with astrologers, with those who can foretell the future by the stars. So we wouldn't want anything to do with astrology either. Moses didn't, and demanded his people have nothing to do with those people who could read the stars.

The understanding of that is this – in the Old Testament, there are four separate and distinct gods being discussed, but we've been unaware of that. This is due to the priesthood who put that Old Testament together, and you weren't there, so you don't know this fact. The priesthood knew that there were four different deities.

One of the four deities was the Sun, or Solar. That is where we get Solomon, King Solomon from. Sol being the Latin for the Sun, Om being Hindu for the Sun, and On was the city of the Sun in Egypt. Sol – Om – On. Just three different names for the same deity. Think of that next time you flip "on" a light switch. So one of the gods in the Old Testament was the Sun. The others were approached through the predominant cults of the time. One was of the stellar cult. The old Hebrew stellar group connected themselves with their God through the stars. Then there was the moon cult, or the lunar cult, of which Moses was the leader. So you have the solar cult, the star cult, and the moon (or lunar) cult accounting for three of those Old Testament gods (we'll get to the fourth one soon).

Moses was the Hebrew leader of the lunar cult, while Jehovah, or Yahweh, was the lunar God. He was El before that, and that goes back into the ancient Semitic, which in turn goes back to the planet Saturn. But Moses, being a worshipper of a lunar God, El, or Jehovah, naturally would not want to have anything to do with the other group across the street or down the block who worshiped a different God, who worshiped the stars. That is why Moses would tell his followers not to have anything to do with the star worshipers. After sundown the moon comes out. That is why Moses would have all the holy days at sundown, because that is when the moon comes out. One of the main reasons why the moon, or the lunar, was worshiped by Moses' followers was because the moon had control over the women's menstrual cycle. Since they were into sex worship, that is one of the primary reasons why they worshiped the moon. The old lunar cults were sex worshipers.

This brings us to the subject of circumcision. Now, what does cutting the foreskin off of a boy's penis got to do with the Lord? It doesn't have a thing to do with the Lord, it has to do with sex. That is why you are messing around with the boy's penis. They had the boys circumcised because they found out that a man would get aroused quicker, without the foreskin than he would with the foreskin. That was not new with the Hebrews, this ritual goes way back to stone age man. The Egyptians did the same thing, preparing boys for a little sex worship.

We now are faced with a new scripture, in the Christian context, with Jesus, or God's Son, saying that in my house are many mansions. The problem with this is that is not the exact translation in the Bible. The King James version mistranslates the Bible a lot. You have to understand why, because the old British, the old Anglo-Saxon British, were not that keen on Hebrew and Greek. They did the best they could, but they still mistranslated a lot. They know that. Originally translated, it should be, "In my Father's abode there are many houses. Well sure, there are at least twelve that we know of – the twelve houses of the zodiac. So, in my Father's abode there are many houses. That's what God's "Sun" was specifying. King James was a wonderful man, I know, but his lackeys just didn't know Hebrew and Greek well enough to translate things correctly.

Later on we see that the Son is betrayed, and of course, He is betrayed by Judas, or Scorpio, being November, or in the Fall of the year. That is when the rays are cut

Jesus depicted with a "crown of thorns," representing the Sun's illumination.

short. Samson's hair is cut short, or the Sun/Son's rays are cut short in the winter, so he dies. What we are talking about, again, is astrology.

We can go back into the ancient world for the understanding of many modern-day concepts, and to understand the Bible and the light of truth. We never quite revealed in the Bible what was always associated with light. The light was also associated with telling the truth about something, and if you have good knowledge on something, then people say that you are brilliant, you are in the light, you are enlightened. As the ancient Egyptians said, if you put the truth out of your mind when someone is giving you the truth, and is showing you the truth, what you are doing is killing the light of truth. It is the same as killing God's Son, the light of truth, when you are killing the truth in your head, in your brain. That is where you are cutting off the light of truth in your mind. Therefore, they said that God's Sun/Son was killed, was put to death on Golgottha – "Skull Place," as they called it. That's where the brain is, in your skull. Skull Place is where you put the truth and the light to death. The light of truth, God's Son, has always been impaled between two thieves. There is regret for the past and fear of the future. We've always put the death of light between two thieves.

The sun has been used by Kings, rulers, potentates – and every kind of ruler and institution worldwide has used it on their flags, emblems, symbols, police badges, just about everywhere. The sun symbol has been used by everybody, that is why it is called King of Kings, Lord of Lords.

The symbolic headdress on the Statue of Liberty represents the Son/Sun with its "crown of thorns" – or rays of the sun.

The sun was said also to have died with a crown of thorns. All you have to do is fly over the statue of liberty to see the crown of thorns, because the crown of thorns is nothing more than the sun's rays. When the sun is dying in the evening you can go out to the ocean and see the sun walking on water. What do you see? You see the sun rays, dying with a crown of thorns. It is also said that the way God's Sun/Son left, is the way that He is coming back. On a cloud. That is usually the way the sun leaves, on a could. Normally, in the morning, if there are some clouds, He comes up on a cloud. The way He left is on a cloud, and the way he returns is on a cloud. The Bible says that every eye is going to see God's Son when He comes back. Well, you have to be dead or blind not to see the sun.

There's a story about God's Son during a storm, the great tempest in the Bible. God's Son was sleeping and the storm was so bad that the men on the ship, the seasoned sailors, just wanted to die, commit suicide, because it was so rough. But God's Son was downstairs in the ship sleeping. Everybody else on the boat is going to die, they are scared to death, and He is sleeping. Now, I have heard about sound sleepers, but a man continues to sleep right through this terrible storm, and He doesn't even hear it raging. Just understand that the Sun does control weather, it controls the storms on the sea because when it comes out, the storms leave. The ancients knew this, they knew that the sun controlled the seas. So this is yet another story about the physical sun, disguised as an interesting parable that will give us all hope about the return of our "savior."

So we see ourselves coming to an end about what Christianity reveals. I just wanted to give a background, to show the astro-theology, or the astrological aspects of the Bible taken from the ancient texts, Egypt in particular, and how these symbols and sayings have developed right into modern day thinking. Also, how this has developed into a political ideology, and leads into some premises, views, and values, and of course, the associations around secret societies.

Now, we will finish up with a few more pertinent relationships to the symbols. One, in particular, is in relationship to the other symbols of the two fishes, which is Pisces, and then the age that is coming up, beyond the year 2000. That is why we are "in the last days." Yes, the last days of Pisces. That's all. It is just that simple, we are coming into the end of an age. That is why we are going to have a new age. They changed the end of the age to the end of the world, for a mistranslation. Just as other mistranslations, they did this purposely.

However, I believe that there is going to be a new age, and it is not the one they planned for us. I think there is someone or something higher than the "high ones" of this world, and there is going to be a new way of doing things. It isn't going to include the kind of manipulation, usury, exploitation, and the kind of stuff coming down for the last two thousand years, because we cannot afford another two thousand years of this stuff. We've got to clean this stuff up!

The age before Pisces was the age of Aries, the Ram. That was when the ancient Hebrews blew the Ram's horn for the beginning of the year. The ram's horn was Aries, the Ram. And out of that comes the ram, or the lamb of God. In the ancient Hebrew they put to death the lamb, because it was called the paschal lamb, the symbol for the age under Aries, the paschal lamb, or ram. Then in the next age we have the bull, when they were worshipping the golden calf. They worshiped the sun as the golden part, and the calf was the bull, or Taurus the bull. So the golden calf represented Taurus the bull.

Then we see the judgment day, when everybody is going to be brought back to life and judged, that is the judgment day. But this is ancient Egyptian, and is just another "story." There has never been a judgment day, that is just a story. Unless you understand what the ancient Egyptians were saying, you'll never know the difference. And that is that the day that you are living right now is your judgment day. You are being judged right now, and if you understand that, then you can go on and not worry yourself sick over what is going to happen to you when you die. You are not going up to heaven with God's Son. I don't know where you are going, but you are quite likely not going up there with God's Son.

The idea that Hell was hot comes from the fact that the sun was hot. In Egypt the sun is hot, a lot hotter than it is in other countries. In Egypt it is hot! They figured that when the sun goes down at night, it must also be hot while it is going through the Earth. So if you die and go into the Earth it must be hot. Of course, when volcanoes blow up hot stuff, that proves that the Earth is hot. So if you go into Hell and you die, you go to Hell, and it is hot. You go into the Earth, it is hot. Actually, the word Hell is Nordic and it was spelled Hel, not Hell. It meant a place where you bury something – like a grave. If you bury something in a hole and cover it up, that is Hel, in the Scandinavian tongue. Therefore, if you put something over your head to cover it, that is a hel – met. Because that is what hel meant, covering something up.

Now let's look at the word blessing. Everybody is looking for a blessing. The word blessing comes from the word blood, or bloedsain, as an English, or Welsh word, blessing or blood, which means the shedding of blood. Any time there is a bloodletting, or killing, or shedding of blood, it was a blessing. That is why the Crusaders couldn't wait to get back to tell the Pope that they had killed all the people, because that was a wonderful blessing. They had shed a lot of blood. This goes back to the ancient world, long before Israel, when the animals would have to be sacrificed and you would have to pour out the blood afterward, and that was a blessing. As a matter of fact, the Earth today has been blessed all over the world. There has been more bloodshed in the name of religion in Ireland, and the Middle East and all over the world. So we are being totally blessed all over the world with this bloodshed. I just happen to think it is an idea whose time has come get rid of these blessings, and go back to school and find out that we've been had!

Anyway, Christians will tell you that they have been bathed in the blood of the lamb. Now, nothing could be more repulsive than to be bathed in the blood of the lamb. But, that is exactly what the high priest in ancient Israel, and the ancient Hebrew religious philosophies would do. They would cut the heads of the lambs off, and then they would drain the blood and sprinkle the blood on the sacrifice and then sprinkle the blood on the people as a great blessing, and then they would sprinkle it on themselves. And, that is *very* holy, until you start to think about it, and see what it looked like to see an old man with blood all over him. That just does not bring up, into my mind, something of holiness. That sounds like animal sacrifice and cruelty to animals. We would get all bent out of shape if we were driving along the street someday and saw some animal with his head cut off and see his blood out in the street. People would think that that was just terrible. But that is what they did in the Bible – just cut some poor animal's head off and drain the blood, and that was a blessing. And that is because we don't know what these words mean. We need to define the terms and educate ourselves as to exactly where our beliefs come from.

Now again, I am an academic, a teacher. I am not a radical, I am not trying to put down religion. I am not trying to, in any way, offend anyone. I am just trying to get to the bottom of things, and incidentally, that is what radical means – someone who is trying to get to the bottom of things. So if that is what I am doing, and I can be classified as a radical from this definition – then I am a radical, because I just want to get down to the bottom of things.

The Mass in Christianity is a celebrating of Christ's blood that was shed from His body. Eating of the body, of the God, is a very old concept, some of the most ancient rituals in the world would worship a God, and cut him up and eat him. As a matter of fact, Baal, in the ancient Semiticor Syrian scheme of things, was a God and they would make a cake to Baal, and cut it up and eat it. They would eat the flesh of Baal. Later on, they liked that so much that they started eating each other. They were from Cana. Therefore, that is where we get what was called the Cana Baal. Cannibal! Because the people of Cana would eat the flesh of Baal. The Cana Baal.

The drinking of the blood always went with the eating of the flesh of the God. That might sound very holy, but what does that look like to us today? Just as Dick Gregory said, if you went home one night and saw your children drinking wine and having bread, having some kind of a feast, and you asked them what they were doing and they said, "Well, we were just drinking some of your blood, and eating some of your flesh." You'd say, "That sounds sick! What are those kids doing?" Well, that is just what these people were doing in ancient times during their sacrificial rituals. They were eating their God's blood, and eating his flesh. These are the sacramental ceremonies that are going on in today's churches. So basically, what I want to say is that the defenders of today's Christianity are called apologists. And does Christianity have a lot to apologize for today? There is no doubt about that. It was once said by an ancient philosopher that allegiance to an old myth never broke a chain, nor freed a human mind.

Most people will hear what they want to hear. They don't want to hear anything they don't agree with. But somewhere along the line, we are going to have to deal with the reality that we are in today. Because no one is leaving this country. Blacks are not leaving this country. Blacks are not leaving this country to go back to Africa, and white folks are not going to leave to go back to England. As a matter of fact, there are more people coming into this country than are ever going to leave. What we are going to have to do is figure out what the problems are and be straight with each other, be honest, and get to the truth – to find out where racism and bigotry comes from, where ignorance comes from, and where this whole idea of dark and black being bad, and the Prince of Darkness. And, of course, the Sun/Son coming up in the morning is the Prince of Light, so that is where we get that old context of dark and light.

Over and above that, I mentioned before that we had four gods in the Old Testament, and I want to throw something in here. There is a lot of good academic material coming out right now from universities throughout the world, and not just in this country. There are some very good academics coming out now to investigate the writing of the Pentateuch and the writings of the Bible. There are a lot of people looking at the possibility that the first five books of the Bible, the Pentateuch, were written by women. Now, if they can prove that, that is going to set everybody back about three years growth. I wasn't there, I don't know, but I see some very good scholarship being developed right now, and some very good material on that subject. There is at least a possibility.

Now, I mentioned before that there were four Gods, but I only mentioned three. So, I am going back over the four again. There was the stellar God, the lunar God, and the solar God, and then, of course, we had Saturn. Saturn is a very interesting fourth God, that is kind of hidden in the scriptures. However, the more you get into the scriptures and check out the words, and the phrases, you begin to see the words that have to do with Saturn.

That is why today, when you get married, you get married before God. And the symbol of that God is the ring that is put on each other's fingers. The ring of Saturn. In the marriage phrases, one also begins to see what that has to do with Saturn. So when you get married, you get married with a ring, and the symbol of that God is the ring, the ring of Saturn. You're wearing God's ring. And the yarmulke was the round ring that you wear on your head, for Saturn your God. Even in the middle ages, in the temples, Catholic monks would shave their heads in a round circle, and the Hebrews, instead of doing that, would wear the yarmulke. But it all had to do with the round rings of Saturn.

Kings would wear round headgear, not that that was more representative of the sun – but because they were higher, or more powerful. Just the kings would wear the round crown of thorns, and the thorns were then turned in and became the king's crown. That is why today, kings rule by "divine right." It was to emulate the Lord, who ruled as "king of kings, and Lord of Lords." Therefore, because they have placed themselves as king, directly under God, they can rule the land. Because they said so. "I am the King, and you are not!" Now, that is the basis for tyranny.

Let's get back to Saturn. Saturn was always pictured as black, incidentally. The ancients assigned black to Saturn, for whatever reason, and the symbol for Saturn was the sickle, like the Russian sickle, and on the tip of the sickle there was a cross. And if you go to the library today, you will see that the astronomical symbol for the planet Saturn was a sickle, with a cross on top. That meant that the cross overcomes the sickle. Think about that. That is interesting. But to get back to Saturn, being the ancient God, El, it was called the Ugaritic God, or the Syrian Ugaritic God, which is what we call today, Palestine. The northern area of Palestine was Syria – and was associated with the God's name, El.

Back then, the area that we call the Middle East today was totally, absolutely under the influence of a more ancient empire, Egypt. In Egypt one of the original divinities was Isis. Isis was a male/female progenitor of knowledge and wisdom, etc. So this was always pictured as a Mother holding a child, which is the same aspect of Mary holding the child. Incidentally, that is where we get the song, *Mary Had a Little Lamb*, because Mary had a little "lamb," the lamb of God, called Jesus.

The Egyptian goddess Isis with a child (Horus), which represented Mary with the baby Jesus years later.

When you look closely, that is where all those nursery rhymes come from in children's myths.

Anyway, Saturn being El, was under the domination of Egypt. That whole area had its philosophies, ideas, and its people being dominated by Egypt. So Isis was the first main divinity. Now, with the coming of Ahknaton, the worship was then changed to the worship of Amen-Ra, the sun. This is where we get sun-ray from – from Amen-Ra. Amen-Ra was worshiped in the temples as God's Sun/Son. At the end of the services they would say Amen, because they were sending a prayer to God through Amen-Ra, God's Sun/Son. So they would say Amen when they sent the prayer through God's Sun/Son. The ancient Egyptians said nobody had seen God, and perhaps, there is nobody who is ever going to see God. But when you have seen the sun, you have seen the Father. And when you pray to the Father, you pray directly to the Father, but you send your prayer through God's sun, Amen-Ra. So at the end of the prayer you say, Amen. God's "son," Amen-Ra, served as a personal savior to them, since it gave them all life.

The symbol that was used in the religious context for Saturn, was the square.

The sacred black cube that Muslims pilgrimage to at Mecca. Black was the color of the planet-god Saturn.

A square, a square box. And, it was black, and that is why Mecca is a great square black box. The home of Mecca is a square, black box. Because it has to do with the symbol of Saturn, which is square. It has nothing to do with black, because of Negro, it has to do simply with assigned color to that particular planet. This is an interesting point in that Central Africa was blessed with a lot of rain, and lower Africa, which was North Africa, had just about no rain. So that was a desert out there, and Central Africa was very high, and the highlands would get lots of rain. In the Spring when the rains would come, the waters would flow both Southward, into South Africa, or into North Africa, which I said was a desert. It would begin to fill up the tributaries and all the rains were flowing into Egypt. So, once a year the Nile would overflow, because it couldn't deal with that volume of water. A great flood would be flowing into Egypt, and they would always refer to it as "the waters of chaos." That was a time of terrible destruction. Well, of course, a flood is a time of destruction.

The "square" was also a symbol associated with Saturn, hence the black mortarboard of college graduates. Of course, mortarboards have played an important role in "masonry" as well.

However, along with that terrible destruction, also came new life. Because if that water doesn't come in, nothing is going to grow, and if you think it is dead now, wait until there is no rain, no Nile – then you are *really* going to be dead in that heat. Therefore, the waters of chaos came, and the destruction of the world occurred in Egypt. Once the water had receded, and had deposited the minerals and nourishment, that would then be the basis of all the new life in Egypt. So they said that Egypt, like you and me, would be "born again." Egypt came out from under the water and was born again with new life.

And they called that celebration the coming of the great flood. The symbol of that celebration was a quarter moon, like a little boat. It looked like a little boat, like a little canoe. It was a quarter moon, the lower quarter of the moon. That lower quarter of the moon in Egypt was known as the word *arghanoa*. The arghanoa was the lower quarter of the moon when the rains came, the monsoon rains.

That is where we get the Ark of Noah, or Noah's Ark. But, it is actually the Egyptian Ark of Noah, which was the wet moon. Noah's Ark. The arghanoa. Then when you get further into Saturn, you begin to understand that his color is black, that he was a God of one of the many different Semitic tribes, or groups, and one of his symbols was a square. Then you get into the square black mortarboard that the university, or high school students wear when they graduate. It is a square on his head, and it is usually black. The color of Saturn, one of the ancient Hebrew Gods. This is the same black used on the robe the judge wears when he is going to throw you in jail. Because the black represents Saturn, Saturn is the old Semitic God. That is why churches and courtrooms look the same today, because when you go into churches you sit out here with the poor folks in the chairs out here in the pews, but you cannot go up onto the lifted higher elevation, you can't go inside the gate, you can't go inside the little doors, only the priest can go inside there and officiate for you. You stay on the outside with the poor folks. The altar is always raised at least three tiers, because in Egypt that was the way it was always done. The altar was always raised so the people could see the representative of God dressed in black. The priest comes out on the altar dressed in black, and he is officiating for you, he is the mediator between you and God. That is the same thing that happens in the courtroom, you walk in and you are part of the poor folks sitting out here in the audience, and here is the fence, or gate, that separates you. The attorneys can go inside the gate and they are your mouthpiece, to go talk to "God" for you and see if they can get you off, and the lawyers will be the mediator between "God," or the "judge" who judges you, and man. That is where all of this comes from in our society today.

The "Sharif" of the ancient world was a lawgiver who was represented by the six-pointed Star of David.

Let's take a look at the word sheriff. This comes from the word *sharif* (like Omar Sharif). A sharif was the lawgiver in the ancient Egyptian world, and his symbol was the six pointed star, or the star of David. That is what the sheriff wears today, the six pointed star. When you get into all of that you open up a whole new realm of thought, because now our symbols on the streets begin to take special meaning when you understand that they come from the ancient Bible. Then you find out who the people were behind the old Bible and you begin to figure things out, and

The ancient symbol of the rising Sun, freeing the world from darkness, can be seen in the corporate logo of Shell Oil.

begin to see how these symbols all connect. Like the shell sign, for Shell Oil Corporation. It is not a shell. Look at it closely. It is the rising sun with its rays extended and is only disguised as a shell. This is *not* a coincidence; I've looked into this. This same rising sun is a popular occult symbol found all over the world, on many flags of countries and other important logos and insignias.

The ARCO logo is a square at first glance, but look again. It is a pyramid seen from above. As we look down on the pyramid, we see that it has no capstone. The same pyramid on the back of the American dollar has no capstone – it is there, but is pictured above the pyramid and is not connected to it. It is from that same vantage point that we look down on the ARCO "pyramid." You'd better do your homework and find out who owns these oil companies.

We've all seen the Exxon sign, but not for much longer since it was just bought by Mobil. Few realize that the Exxon logo actually represents the "double-cross" of freemasonry, and we all know how it feels to be double-crossed.

The flag of Antigua (and many other countries) incorporates the rising sun symbolism into its national identity.

Let me explain more about the ARCO symbol. In the Bible, the twelve apostles are called the twelve cor-

The "double-cross" of Freemasonry can be seen in the corporate logo of the now-defunct Exxon.

nerstones of the church. Jesus is also referred to in the Bible as "the Chief Cornerstone that the builders rejected." The Chief Cornerstone is a Greek word that means "the peak of a pyramid," – the tip of the pyramid at the top is a "chief cornerstone." So stop for a minute, and think about the message being so very subtly delivered by the ARCO company. Who is in charge of world, really in charge, without the "chief cornerstone" being here? Who owns the oil companies? And who owns *you*??

Now let's talk about Steven Spielberg's movie, "The Raiders of the Lost Ark." They are raiding the lost ark, but if you go to the encyclopedia, or any library and get *Smith's Bible Dictionary*, page 23, under the heading of ark, you will see a beautiful ark. It says the ark was the Egyptian ark, was made in Egypt, and was purely an Egyptian idea. Now you can understand why Spielberg's movie took place in Egypt, with Anglo/American white folks looking for the lost ark with Nazis, who are also looking for it. The Nazis represent Europe, as Europe is the "old world," along with "new world" Americans who are also looking for the ark. Where are those two cabals looking, Hitler and Indiana Jones? They are looking in Egypt. They are not looking in Israel, they are not looking in Jerusalem. They are looking in Egypt because that is where the ark came from, and they know it. But see, they haven't fully explained that to you in the film – it goes right over the heads of most people. Many, many answers regarding religion and its origins go back to Egypt.

Now, it is true that there is something to this idea of the lost ark, and the holy grail – and Spielberg's movie of the lost ark, along with the next one, "Indiana Jones and the Temple of Doom," provides clues. If you can't understand those two, then you sure can't understand the last one, "Indiana Jones and the Last Crusade." The last crusade. Now, if you can't understand the first crusade in the Middle Ages, you are not going to understand the last crusade. Because it is the same crusade, and it's been going on for a long time. That crusade is very simple, and I am going to explain that to you.

Jesus was referred to as the "chief cornerstone" that the builders rejected. A chief cornerstone is the peak of a pyramid. ARCO's corporate logo represents the missing chief cornerstone from an aerial view of the Great Pyramid.

These crusades are between some very powerful secret societies in the world, that make the Mafia look like Sunday school. They are very powerful criminal secret societies in this world, and they would just scare you to death. And, they are at work in our world today. They are battling for the Holy Grail. The Holy Grail was a cup, and according to the ancient teachings, the cup was the Earth. The cup is the Earth of life, that holds all life, and the cup holds all the blood. The blood on Earth is in the Holy Grail, so whoever controls the Earth, controls the Holy Grail and controls all the holy blood. The holy blood is in the Holy Grail. Now, that goes back to this old idea about the shedding of the blood. Why are we going to shed the blood? Well, we are going to shed the blood to gain control. And, that will be our blessing. That's right, you are going to get blessed with the shedding of all this blood. The cup is the Earth and the blood is you. Now we can understand what they mean by the New World Order, and the methods that are being used to accomplish it.

We should understand that there are some very powerful secret societies that are operating in the world that you have never heard of, because anytime you hear of anything going on in this world, you can be rest assured that it isn't important. Because if you have heard of it, it isn't important. It is what you haven't heard about that is going to scare you! Now, we are getting into something that is quite pertinent to this whole discussion.

We can look around the world and see that we have nothing but problems. We're talking about war, racism, and dissension between peoples throughout the world. What causes this? Big business makes money from major conflicts and we should look carefully as to who owns these major businesses. The rule applies that only a few have control over the many, and these few are quite often connected to secret societies and big money. The major films in Hollywood sometimes give us clues because these same large companies own the film studios.

There's been a lot of information coming out in movies about these secret fraternal orders. "Godfather III" deals with a secret society of Freemasons operating out of the Vatican. But that's not exactly where Freemasonry operated during the beginnings of the Vatican back in the Third and Fourth Century. They weren't around yet. Other power groups often influenced the Vatican, and religious institutions were merely outward fronts for the power groups in control. We've always known – and have seen it in our own country – that the many public organizations, institutions, and churches are just "fronts" for those who hold the power. The front organizations always operate in the light of day, while behind them exists the money, and the real power behind the scenes. It always goes back to money, because money is power.

Those who want information on the secret organizations behind the Vatican might go to the library and look in the Encyclopedia Britannica or any other good reference book and look under The Knights of Malta. If you want to get into American religions, look under the York Rite movements of Freemasonry. A classic example is Charles Taze Russell, a founder of the International Bible Students, later to become known as the Jehovah's Witnesses. Russell himself was a York Rite Mason. He went to England and met with Louis, of the House of Rothschild, and with the Zionist leaders. Later, he came back to America and promoted what he called Jehovah's Witnesses, and their concept of a New World Order. They have been preaching in America for over one hundred years about a New World Order, the same New World Order that we hear about today. That's the same New World Order that President Bush was speaking about publicly. This is the same New World Order the Mormons are talking about in their gatherings. This the same New World Order that the Seventh Day Adventists are looking forward to realizing.

It is interesting how all of these groups just mentioned clearly use Masonic symbols that are closely tied in with their organizations. If the "New World Order" should come down upon us, many changes will be made. It seems these religious groups – the Mormons, Seventh Day Adventists, and Jehovah's Witnesses – are all vying to be the religion that takes over along with the New World Order. Some of the same Masonic symbols that they use were put on the American dollar bill in 1934. These are Federal Reserve notes, and these symbols were put on the Federal Reserve notes by Franklin D. Roosevelt. He may not have taken credit for this, however, by writing a private letter to a friend named Colonel House, on November 21st, 1933. He told the Colonel, "The real truth of the matter is, as you and I know, that a financial element in the larger centers has owned the Government ever since the days of Andrew Jackson."

FDR, according to his own son-in-law, was manipulated from day one. Curtis Dall wrote a book called *My Exploited Father-in-Law*. In it, he stated, "For a long time I felt that FDR had developed many thoughts and ideas that were his own to benefit this country, the United States. But, he didn't. Most of his thoughts, his political ammunition, as it were, were carefully manufactured for him in advanced by the Council on Foreign Relations–One World Money group. Brilliantly, with great gusto, like a fine piece of artillery, he exploded that prepared "ammunition" in the middle of an unsuspecting target, the American people, and thus paid off and returned his internationalist political support.... The One World Government leaders and their ever close bankers have now acquired full control of the money and credit machinery of the U.S. via the creation of the privately owned Federal Reserve Bank."

Franklin Roosevelt, as history tells us, instituted a plan that was called "The New Deal." The New Deal ultimately revealed that we used to be America, but that "our enterprise was now a success." (This is based on this new money at the time – stated to this day on the back of the one dollar bill, in Latin.) In effect, they were saying, "We have changed America from being a free enterprise system and have now brought into world banking the IMF, The International Monetary Fund. And we have total success over the American people, over the American economy and the American people never even knew what happened to their rights." That's why many of the cults and movements across America are promoting a New World Order. They are all welcoming the new Millennium, and attempting to position themselves should changes occur. The Pat Robertson's of the world (he's a prominent Christian evangelist), from all the Christian broadcasting radio and television programs are welcoming the new Millennium because the Lord is coming back. Excuse me, but the Lord is *supposed to be* coming back. The new Millennium begins a new one-thousand year period that they think has some significant connection to Bible prophecy. I know this much. The Lord might not be coming back, but you'd better keep an eye out for that New World Order. They're going to need an official religion, you know. And in many ways, the New World Order is already here. The cement is hardening around your feet – you just don't know it yet. Just try to move, and exercise some of the freedoms you *thought* you had. Many of our freedoms have already disappeared.

Christianity is a Freemasonic concept. Many Freemasonic concepts originated in Egypt. Freemasonry did not officially exist yet during early Christianity in the way we know it today, but Christianity is based on Freemasonic concepts and ideas established partly by Egyptians and partly by the old Essenes that lived in Middle East. That is why, incidentally, that we had so many problems getting the *Dead Sea Scrolls* out, because, in my opinion, there is material in the *Dead Sea Scrolls* that can cause some very serious problems with Christianity and Judaism. Much of the *Scrolls* have been released, but few people are studying what they really say. And contrary to what you might think, not all of the *Dead Sea Scrolls* have been released. As of this writing, one book, *The Angel Scroll*, remains under lock and key in monastery Germany. What remains hidden could be damaging to those belief systems, and there may be a vested interest in keeping it locked away.

I am not condemning anyone of the Christian or Jewish faiths. I am only presenting the factual records of history. It is time that we become open to looking at all of our backgrounds, and where we came from, and come to understand that we all have things that we need to know about our origins.

We are told that the New Testament came from the teachings of Jesus Christ. But Christianity is also the retelling of the most ancient story the world has ever known. The story of Christianity itself, as it has come down to us, about the one that Christianity calls the Christ, or Jesus, is not the same Jesus that walked on the Earth. There is a big difference between the idea in our mind of the Jesus of Christianity, as taught to us, and the actual authentic Jesus that walked on the Earth. That's why today Jews do not accept Jesus as the Christ, or the Messiah. They were the ones in the Middle East, it was their country, their language and their book. If they don't accept the story, there must be a reason why. The Hebrews do not accept the story of Jesus as being true. Here we have a religion that supposedly originated in their own country using their own language, and they do not accept it. Whatever the ancient Hebrews were individually, or as a people, they were not stupid. They were and are very well educated. However, they do not accept the story of Christianity. So, if they are not accepting this story, I would like to know why.

Now, my outcome is that I understand why. I have run this by many times with Rabbis in the field of theology, the clergy. I now know that what I know, they know. Basically, what the Jews will tell you, and they are right, is that there was a man named Jesus, but that the name Christ was just a title, and he did not have this title during his life. Christ. His name was not Jesus Christ, it was Jehoshua Ben-Pandira, which is in the old Talmud, it's in Jewish literature, and Jews know about this man Jesus. However, he lived about one hundred years before the Jesus of the New Testament would have lived. The "Jesus of Nazareth" lived about one hundred years before the one that we read about in the Bible. Modern scholarship now tells us that the town of Nazareth did not only *not* exist during Jehoshua Ben-Pandira's lifetime – it did not yet exist during the lifetime attributed to the New Testament Jesus, either. There is much in the New Testament does not pan out. The entire story in the New Testament was written in such a way as to tell us a metaphysically encoded story. It is the greatest *story* ever told, not a collection of facts, but a story.

I am not saying this story is bad, it has a lot of merit, but it is a metaphysical parable, it is a symbolic story. The story comes from God, but was contaminated when man got a hold of it and destroyed the whole principle, by getting involved with money, instead of with loving, and with God. The story itself is a very enlightening story that needs to be told, as long as you understand what is actually being related. There is a message that is encoded in the scriptures, both in the New Testament, as well as the Old Testament. Encoded in such a way that there is another deeper story revealed within the Bible itself.

So what do I mean by "encoded?" In the military, or other intelligence organizations, a message might be received to relay critical data. The message says one thing, but if you take every sixth letter from the message and put them together, the receiver has a completely different message. One message is encoded within another. That is what I'm saying about the Bible, both the Old and the New Testaments. I'm not talking about things like that cryptic book, *The Bible Code*. That has since been intelligently discredited. I'm talking about plain English, properly translated, and reading what's directly in front of you. It's there, but most people fail to see it because they are taking things either too literally, or are accepting blindly what they've been told to believe, without thinking for themselves. All it takes is to look closely, and to *think*. Anyone can read the message of Jesus, but only a few unknown people can read the encoded message. Not only do I see it, but I've talked with many experts about this and they assure me this is true.

That's what I am saying here, and that is why the Jews do not accept this biblically written story of the New Testament Jesus, because they are very smart in this field of Semitic theology and they know the encoded message. Now, why the story was written in an encoded form, I don't know. I guess you would have to talk to God to understand the answer to this monumental question. Most likely, the Divine presented this information in such a way that you have to put out something yourself to get the message. You are not going to just get it, like you go to Sears, you have to really want that understanding. You are not going to receive this understanding by just opening a vein, and popping an IV, you have to really want to acquire this meaning behind the writing.

Seek and ye will find, knock and it will be opened unto you, ask and ye will receive. Ask and it will be given unto to you. The whole idea is to study and prove all things, don't just accept the way things are, until you have done so. Hold fast to that which is true. The whole idea is for you to do your homework. Don't expect someone to appear and lead you to God. That will never happen, it is not happening now, and it is never going to be that easy.

Symbols and emblems are the bottom line of any revelations. If you don't know how to read the symbols, you wont know what the story is truly about.

Why don't our world religious leaders discuss all these hidden agendas, why don't they reveal the truth about these symbols? Religion and politics are one and the same thing. We have been misled by our misleaders – separating religions from state, we all thought that this had already occurred. Not so! There has never been a political movement on the face of the Earth that wasn't a little religious. By the same token there has never been a religious movement that wasn't somewhat political, and they affect each other more deeply than you could possibly imagine.

In America we have a political institution running our government. Our government is as religious as the Ayatollah Khomeini was, or Saddam Hussein, or any other government of the world, including the Royalty of England. The great royalty of the British people is nothing more than politics. Getting back to the United States government here, the President, the Congress, the legislative branch, the executive branch, the judicial branch – all are religiously based. They all operate within this hidden agenda of symbols and emblems. I am not saying that every one of these people involved in the politics of government is aware of this agenda, but there are the few at the top levels that know and hold this control over the general population. On the surface there are the politicians and there is the clergy. But, the fraternal orders and secret societies, Masonic orders, of sorts, are operating behind the scenes. This is where the clergy can get together with the politicians at their fraternal lodge halls and talk over business, as to who is going to back whom during the political elections. There is a very important connection between politics and religion in America. Let me give you an example.

Someone I know has a friend who was married to a member of the Bohemian Society. This is a group of men who form a huge gathering for what they call the Bohemian Grove "picnic" in Northern California, once a year during the last two weeks of July. During this time, they open the Bohemian Grove up for *one day only* to the member's wives for an assembly of very costly activities. When arriving, everyone is picked up in trams, just like riding into Disneyland. The man driving the tram she rode in on, was black. After attending the event, everyone is then picked up on a tram once again to be returned to their vehicles, which must be left a long distance from the main Grove compound. All during the day of festivities she saw *no* other people of color, *no* other races, whereupon, she had to assume that this was the one "token" black allowed on the grounds of the Grove. She also determined by attending some of the day's events, that the primary attendees were either graduates from the higher institutions of learning, representing only such universities as Yale, Harvard, the University of California, or Stanford. Is this a "picnic," or what really does go on during these summer productions! She also learned that a number of prostitutes were the only females allowed into the compound. But you would usually never hear of this information, unless someone had actually been present and experienced what she revealed to me. Perhaps someone should infiltrate this fraternal order, just as they have done throughout the ages with other righteous groups, to find out the truth of what their primary hidden agenda is all about. Only the most politically and professionally powerful are ever asked to join this all men's club. Think about it!

On another occasion, when she attended as a dinner guest in a stately Tiburon estate, the female hostess began what became a rather intense conversation with those present regarding the fact that women are *never* allowed to enter the hallowed halls of the Bohemian Club, which is located in a prestigious uptown building in the city of San Francisco. The hostess proposed that a class action suit be served upon this club for sexual discrimination. My friend reported that she replied with these words, "Most probably, not in a hundred years, would this 'good ol' boy's club' *ever* allow the rule to exclude women to be changed, in women's favor of being included inside this all male domain." There followed a *very* heated discussion among the rest of the men, who were all members, of course, of the Bohemian Society, and the women present.

Another time, when my friend went to pick up her former husband from a meeting at the Bohemian Club, while waiting for him to appear, there emerged two men dressed in complete drag, with makeup, female attire, the whole effeminate regalia. When she asked about this episode, she was harshly brushed off by her then husband to, "Mind her own business!" Later, she learned that the men dress and enact all female parts during the Grove's annual "picnic" programming, as they prepare very highly designed sets, costumes, and whatever else was necessary to present a richly created production. For these most opulent entertainment productions, which cost thousands and thousands of dollars, the most famous male stars are included, along with many of the national corporate presidents from the film and television industries. This is provided for these men to enjoy during these two weeks of totally affluent associations. These are extraordinarily organized times for major connections for the most powerful men in America today. Needless to say, *every male member* involved is white, upper class, elitist, and highly educated.

I have color pictures of all the ex-Presidents of the United States at the time, standing in unison on a platform, which I understand now is a professionally designed stage-set, before a bonfire, with a large – approximately twenty-five, to thirty foot high owl – with each one of the President's in a cape similar to what you would see at a Ku Klux Clan gathering. This is a specific fraternal order that they belong to and support, to worship an owl as the symbol of wisdom. They do this at twelve midnight. Now, I have to ask you, what are ex-Presidents of the United States, such as Jimmy Carter, Richard Nixon, Gerald Ford, Ronald Reagan, and George Bush doing there? These are all living President's – standing there in unison, the whole line of them, in uniforms, looking like Ku Klux Clan members, in front of a great bonfire, worshipping an owl. And of course, we've all seen the owl which overlooks the front side of the dollar bill, upon its perch in the upper-right hand corner.

In many articles about these goings-on, the research has revealed that the owl symbolizes wisdom, because the owl sees things in the dark. The implication is that these leaders of ours know something that you do not know, thereby symbolizing wisdom, because the owl "sees," knows something, that you do not. The inference here is that there is something going on here in this country. And there is no doubt in my mind that we have no control here in this country. We all have to know that by now.

However, the bottom line is that *people* are the power of the government. The people have always had the power. How would you like to be the King of Perdonia, or some other unknown, insignificant state, with seven hundred subjects, talking to the King of China? There is a terrible differential here. It is the amount of people that the government has under its control, that is where the power comes from in

The front of the American dollar bill reveals a hidden owl in the upper-right hand corner (inset below). This particular bill also has an interesting serial number.

America, and the world. That is where the power truly comes from, it is the *people* that have the power! That is the bottom line. Do the people really want a New World Order? Look at what happened in Seattle in late 1999 with the World Trade riots. Maybe that will tell you. Let's first go back to April, 1994, and look at part of a full-page advertisement run by the government of Morocco in The New York Times. In it, it announced the formation of the World Trade Organization by stating:

> The Final Act of the Uruguay Round, marking the conclusion of the most ambitious trade negotiation of our century, will give birth – in Morocco – to the World Trade Organization, the third pillar of the New World Order, along with the United Nations and the International Monetary Fund.

Most of the those who rioted in Seattle just wanted to have secure jobs and feed their families. However, a few may have known why the WTO was started in the

This inset shows the position (at the center of the picture) of the all-seeing owl as found on the front of the American dollar bill.

first place, as part of this New World Order, and didn't agree with it. The people shut down the meetings, had them cancelled (although temporarily). People can make a difference, but only if they are educated, act together, and refrain from violent acts. Violence gives a bad name to any movement, no matter how elevated in principal, so I'm not advocating riots. If the people, say three and a half million people converge on downtown Los Angeles, shutting down all freeways – black, white, red, yellow – that amount of people demanding that the Mayor come out from his office and go out before the public to sign something today, right now, sign something that the people demand – he would do it, you can bet your boots he'll do it, because the people are demanding it. If the people are demanding it, and the politicians know that if the people are upset, give them what they want. Like Caesar said, give them bread and circuses. Make sure they are diverted with plenty of alcohol, pacified with football games, basketball games, they've got Michael Jordan out there, and make sure they have liquor stores on every corner. Make sure they've got plenty of dope, that they don't even have to go out to get any and bring it home. When you are going to rape something, it is better if you dope them up beforehand. You drug them. So, that is why we are being drugged, make sure they have plenty of alcohol, plenty of entertainment, because somebody is getting ready to do a number on us. We have been led into this with our eyes wide open, just as emotionally and mentally numbed out as they can arrange.

Now this is a very important point I'd like to make here, again. As of this writing, some of the people that placed the money, the brains, and the power behind Adolph Hitler are still alive. And those that *aren't* still alive have passed this job down to their relatives. They keep it in the family. They are still alive and they are still working, putting something together called the New World Order. The New World Order of today is the same one that Adolph Hitler was talking about establishing with his "new order." The New World Order is well on its way. Ronald Reagan did not go to Bitsburg to honor our war dead – it ended up being a Nazi burial plot, and the Jews got a little upset. If I had been a Jew, I would have been out of my mind that the President of the United States is going to Germany to a Nazi burial site, in his words, "To honor the war dead." There is a message in that, and you had better find out what was being connected. You had better find out.

The Vatican turned its head during the Second World War, when the Jews were being put into Nazi concentration camps, and there were connections between Mussolini, the Vatican, and Japan. There are secret societies in the world that have profound power over us, and our politicians know about it. They understand it, and they say nothing because it is too frightening and dangerous for them to deal with it publicly. More than one politician has died mysteriously for sticking his nose where it doesn't belong.

All the Senators, and all the Congressmen have to know about these connections. Somebody had to blow the whistle, and finally someone did. Adam Clayton Powell, the first black Congressman from New York, a brilliant man blew the whistle on the *David Frost Show* many years ago. He died right after that, and he knew he would. He even said he was going to be killed on this television show. Many other people have, and I could give you names of Senators or Congressmen who have spoken about this hidden agenda.

> *The drive of the Rockefellers and their allies is to create a one-world government combining supercapitalism and Communism under the same tent, all under their control.... Do I mean conspiracy? Yes I do. I am convinced there is such a plot, international in scope, genera - tions old in planning, and incredibly evil in intent.*
>
> —Congressman Larry P. McDonald, 1976, killed in the Korean Airlines 747 that was shot down by the Soviets

We have tremendous problems in our country and they're never going to get straightened out, because the real problem is behind the scenes. Our media is not telling us anything – the classic idea of what I am talking about with the media is on the back of the one dollar bill. The eye at the top of the dollar bill is the same eye that is portrayed on the CBS television symbol. CBS is the all-seeing eye, and it goes back to a group of Freemasons that came to this country before the founding of our constitution, who were called the Colombians, known as the Colombian faction. They founded what we know as Columbia University. Out of that has come Columbia space shuttle, Columbia Pictures, and Columbia Broadcasting, CBS, with the all-seeing eye on the pyramid as their symbol. As a matter of fact, our government, our so-called government, is not even a part of our country. It is in an area called the District of *Columbia*. It is a separate district, not part of America at all. The simple truth behind that fact, is that there was a section of the geography in this country that was set aside by a very powerful group of Freemasons, called the Colombian faction, working behind the scenes during the founding of this country.

Who are the Freemasons? This fraternity is connected to levels that go higher and higher and higher (most members don't know this). It just keeps escalating as it goes up. There is an enormous international building in Switzerland that is divided into three parts, which looks like the Mercedes emblem – with the triangle within the circle. That is what this building looks like, a three part building. One third of this building is the United Nations world headquarters, and this is operating in Switzerland. Many people think that the United Nations world headquarters is located in New York. It is not true, it is their field headquarters that is in New York. The main United Nations organization is based in Switzerland, where the banks are located. Then the International Monetary Fund, or the world bankers is in the other third of this building, and the last third belongs to the Freemasons. This was the set up for many years, but as I now understand it, one these groups has since moved out. But the point is for you to understand who is running things at the highest levels in world affairs, and why it's been so important to have all three organizations in the same building for many, many years together. It's a matter of convenience for those who hold the true power.

Do you remember the television show called *Mission Impossible?* If you ever see a rerun, watch the opening of the show very closely. What will come up on the screen will be the insignia IMF – supposedly standing for the "Impossible Mission Force." The impossible mission force, the IMF, the *International Monetary Fund.* What were they always doing on the show? They were always tricking leaders out of positions of authority, assassinating somebody, helping people escape, or doing some other dirty deal, all in a war for power. Whose power? Of course, they were always working for some government, but the agents are not supposed to know who that is for sure.They just do their jobs, not knowing who's really hired them. The "IMF" just sends them out on as mission that they must perform, at all costs. And if anyone should find out who's really pulling the strings, then the agents are told that "we are going to disavow any connection to you." Well, that is the IMF. The International Monetary Fund, which is the power behind the Federal Reserve System, which is raping our country and destroying our economy. And these guys are doing it right in front of you, telling you what they are doing, but we just don't see it. Even after they spell it out for us on television. They are even making comedies about it, like *Get Smart.* On one side you have Chaos, and the other side you have Control. And when you watch the show closely, and ignore the foolishness, it is easy to see that the same operation is running both sides. Creating chaos, then rushing in to "control" it, in order to accomplish an agenda. That is how it has *always* been done. GET SMART! They are telling you something.

Freemasonry's symbol and motto is *Ordo Ab Chao*, meaning "Order out of Chaos." It's found in any reference book. So I am saying that there is a world movement that is financing, organizing, and directing world chaos. Wars, racism, trouble in Northern Ireland, may well be caused by opposing Masonic Orders, between England and the Irish mobs, the syndicates. The Mafia itself is an order of Freemasonry. Sound crazy? The Mafia was connected with the secret societies founded by Giuseppe Messini and Garibaldi, and Albert Pike of the Scottish Rite – it is purely a Masonic Order run like a family of Masonic families.

That is what we have going on in the world today. Masonic families in Europe, the old Hapsburg families, the Rothschilds, the Ottomans. They are ancient families that are power groups, that have controlled world power for thousands of years. They are continuously vying for power, although the new thing at this stage is now this New World Order, which came into existence two hundred years ago in Southern Germany. So I am saying that all of these things that we are watching on the world stage have been intricately organized and directed from behind the scenes. And we, the American people, haven't got the faintest idea in the world of what is happening to us as free citizens.

There are three kinds of citizens in America. However, the people of America have only been told about one. We have purposely been kept ignorant about the other two. The first citizenship that a person can hold in this country is to be a citizen of the United States. That is what we are all told that we should be. There is a second one, and that is to be a citizen of the United States of America, which is totally different. A legally, constitutionally established difference in a court of law. If you are citizen of the United States, you are not a citizen of the United States of America. When you understand that this country was founded and the constitution was written, it was based on something called international maritime admiralty law. We call this law today, world law. The World Court is what the United Nations operates under and is international maritime admiralty law today. Our government was founded as a business corporation, as a company. All corporate law says that you have to have a president and a vice president. That is why we have a President and a Vice President. We are told that we have the right to elect, and that is true, but we don't have a right to *select*, because the corporations decide who is going to run the business. We are experiencing that dilemma right now, in that we can elect, but we cannot select. There is a very real difference in where the power is, and in thinking we know what is going on in our national elections. We have been given the candidates that the corporations selected, of whom they want us to elect.

The entire establishment in America is a business, and you cannot imagine the heads of General Motors or Ford Motor Company getting up in the morning, having a cup of coffee, and wondering what are we going to do today, how are we going to run business today. These powerful male figures have to know what they are going to do twenty years from today, how much oil there is going to be, how much glass will be available, how many people are going to be buying cars. They have to be able to project what the economy will be like twenty years from now, because they have a million or more people on the payroll, so they had better do their homework. They are controlling the whole thing, and our government operates in the same way. They already know who is going to be President, they already know where we will be headed. As a matter fact, someone who was very bright figured this out. You can go back every four years to many of the encyclopedias that were printed the year before the Presidential elections, to that edition, and read that the President is already listed by name in the encyclopedia almost a year before the elections. How do they do this? In late Spring, when the encyclopedias are printed, it already shows the President that is going to be elected in that Presidential year, and he isn't going to be elected until the Fall of that year. He is already there. Nobody's caught that. But many of our encyclopedias and dictionaries come from a secret society of Freemasons in the south of France. Three hundred years ago they were called the *encyclopedia dictionaire*, or the old Knights Templar of France, and they were the enemies of the Roman Church. They were the great progenitors of what we call the Age of Enlightenment, the *encyclopedia dictionaire*. Most

Freemasons know about this, they were the ones that gave us the encyclopedias and dictionaries, that is why they can tell you who is going to be President the year before he is elected, as it comes out in print in the Spring.

We think that our leaders are so wonderful, you had better take a long look at the rest of the story. This includes all the world leaders, as well. All the leaders of the world governments know there is a game going on, a paternal system of power, and it is called loosely, the New World Order. As opposed to the Old World Order. It's the new game in town, and it's taking over. Better get in line.

Europe dominated the world, so Europe was called the Old World, and, of course, included the powers behind it. The old European families, the Masonic secret societies behind these powerful old families, the Romanoffs, the Krupps – they were the power groups, working in unison, a power unit called Europe, which dominated the world. The Vatican dominated Europe together with these families, but today the New World Order is slowly eroding that power away from the old world. It is a massive and complex struggle that we never see on the surface.

So where is this New World Order based out of? It is based in Britain and America. But it is mainly British. There is a big difference between being English and British, totally different. It is a night and day difference, as English is a blood-line coming out of the old Celtic peoples of the Nordic race, while British means "man of the covenant," or "holy man," as I had previously explained.

Prince Charles is never going to become King because he would not go along with the scheme of things there, so their breaking up his marriage and making him look like a dope is the result of that. It seems clear that his first son is going to be King. The powers that be do not want Charles to be King. Prince Andrew is the Duke of York, which is the head of the York Rite of England, which is working in concert with New York, the Empire State. It does appear that Prince Andy is not going along the way he should, so his marriage has been broken up and he is also being made to look like a fool. Behind those two men are very powerful secret societies.

> *The governments of the present day have to deal not merely with other governments, with emperors, kings and ministers, but also with the secret societies which have everywhere their unscrupulous agents, and can at the last moment upset all the governments' plans.*
> —British Prime Minister Benjamin Disraeli, 1876

So to this day, very little has changed. What do we do now, where do we go with all this information, this hidden agenda that incorporates so many world secrets as to boggle the average mind? Keep in mind now that what we are talking about is the Old World Order of Europe. Adolph Hitler was secretly financed, organized, and directed out of America by big business to destroy the Old World Order of Europe – to cause havoc in the other guy's back yard. This is now a proven fact. When Hitler had accomplished what he was supposed to do, then American industry cut off his oil, cut off all of his supplies, and Hitler went under. Now understand that America is in the hands of what we call in America, the New World Order. Hitler, of course, was kept in the dark as to this hidden agenda. He was a pawn in the game. So the industrial complex power mongers used him until their ultimate goal was accomplished at that time.

What is their ultimate goal today? Their ultimate goal is to bring about God's Kingdom. Prince Charles, or whomever is going to be King, will be sworn in by the Arch Bishop of Canterbury and will make this new King repeat after him these words, "When you accept this position as King of England for Jehovah, for the God of the Old Testament, you are sitting on the throne of David for Jesus Christ, until such time that Jesus comes back, you are King of God's Kingdom. The Pope in Rome says, hey, there is something wrong here, I am suppose to be the Vicar of

Christ. That is why you have the great power struggle between the Old World of Rome, under the Pope, and the New World, under England and America. Who is going to be King of God's Kingdom? Well, as a matter of fact, there is no God's Kingdom – at least on Earth – this is politics at the highest possible level. What we are talking about are churches and government on this side of the Atlantic connected with churches and government in England. What you end up with is a master conspiracy here. There is something very big going on here, our economy is involved and we had better wake up.

In the next century, nations as we know it will be obsolete; all states will recognize a single, global authority. National sovereignty wasn't such a great idea after all.

—Strobe Talbot, President Clinton's Deputy Secretary of State, as quoted in Time, July 20th, 1992.

We shall have world government whether or not you like it, by con - quest or consent.

—Statement by Council on Foreign Relations (CFR) member James Warburg to The Senate Foreign Relations Committee on February 17th, 1950

The people of this country need to wake up and quit depending on the churches to lead you, or depending on the great institutions of great learning to teach you the truth. They are all set up by the power mongering masters of our world. If this country, if not the world, is going to be saved then people must respond from the ground up, at a grass roots level. Individual people, by educating themselves, their families, close friends and associates are waking up to find out that, no, the government is not always going to take care of them. We have to stand on our own, and become thoroughly informed, and damn it, take back the country and our freedom from the powers that be.

PART TWO

The real rulers in Washington are invisible, and exercise power from behind the scenes.
—Supreme Court Justice Felix Frankfurter, 1952

Jordan Maxwell is an author, teacher and lecturer on ancient religions. He has appeared on three CBS-TV specials, ANCIENT MYSTERIES OF THE BIBLE, Parts One and Two, and ANCIENT MYSTERIES OF THE WORLD. Mr. Maxwell is interviewed here by Paul Tice, a writer and Gnostic minister from the San Diego area. This interview first appeared under the title of *On Religion and Politics*.

ON RELIGION AND POLITICS INTERVIEWS PART 1

PT: Some people may not know of your work. Who is Jordan Maxwell?

JM: I feel as though I am an ordinary man in the grips of an extraordinary idea; an ordinary human in pursuit of extraordinary knowledge. The knowledge that I have acquired began when I was very young. My mother's uncle worked at the Vatican, Secretary of State's office, and when he would come back to this country for a visit, he would sit for hours and talk to my family about secret societies, subversive movements, the political intrigue going on behind religious movements, and he used to dazzle me with the explanations about symbols and emblems of occult societies. So I grew up around that kind of knowledge. My grandfather was a Congressman from the state of Florida and there were federal judges in the family, so I grew up hearing things that government figures talk about behind the scenes, with their family, which is a world of difference from what they say publicly. As I grew, I continued to research these hidden areas. I've been waiting for years for someone to deal with these specific subjects that are not normally dealt with. And since no one else has volunteered to do it, I feel a responsibility to speak up.

PT: Most of your work is related to religion, although some family members have been involved in politics. What is the connection between religion and politics?

JM: If you go back into the furthest part of history, as far back as you can go, religion and politics were one and the same. In the ancient world there was never a difference. The king or head of the tribe was always mediator between God and his people. There's never been a political movement in the world that wasn't a little religious, and there's never been a religious movement anywhere that wasn't a little political. Knowing this helps us to understand the connections that can be made today, in our society.

PT: So in our society you're saying that this separation of church and state exists on a more broad or general level, but that behind the scenes there may not be quite so much of a separation there?

JM: Absolutely. There virtually is no separation of church and state – because, for instance, you cannot get married unless you get a marriage license. You can get married before God as long as you have a license from the state. You cannot start a church without first getting government documents, licenses, permits. In the West, generally speaking, the political institutions were founded by the same political establishments that founded religious movements. So religion and politics are, in fact, one and the same thing.

PT: But the main thrust of your work seems to involve religion more than politics. Why?

JM: I prefer to focus more on religion, but politics is equally important. Let's look at the big picture. What I am working to accomplish is to make people aware that man-made institutions, government and religious, are nothing more than a way to control you. To control how you think, to control where you go, how you view things, and what you believe. Man-made churches and governments were meant to control you. So you have a responsibility, not only to your own spiritual self (to educate yourself, spiritually, and take back your life from the hands of your masters), but you also have a responsibility to your Creator. The divine entity who created you and gave you life, gave all creation freedom. Throughout nature, the birds and animals have total freedom. There is a freedom throughout the universe. The only place where we have a lack of freedom is in the human realm. We are the ones who are in prison, and 90 per cent of it is our own fault. We have allowed other people – our churches, our governments, our institutions, to do our thinking for us. And I'm saying that we are moving into a new time, whether we like it or not, where the people all over the Earth are going to have to break free from all the institutions and realize that we are all creations of God and we all have freedoms. We should have the same freedoms that all other creations have. Until such time that we get off of our knees and stand on our feet, and think for ourselves, we will not have the freedom that we were born to have

PT: You pick out Christianity, quite often, as a focal point for this needed change. In what areas do you feel that Christianity is lacking?

JM: Lacking or not, the age of Christianity is on its way out. Christianity, in the last 1600 years (since being formalized), has been symbolized by the two fishes of Pisces. In astrology, you'll find that each governing power was originally called "The Lord" over the constellation it represented. Jesus, "The Lord," was made to represent the two fishes, but we're now entering into another time called the "Age of Aquarius." In the Book of Luke 22:10 where the 12 apostles, or the 12 signs of the zodiac, are asking God's "Sun," the light of the world, where he will go after he leaves the constellation of Pisces, the two fishes, God's Sun says you will go into the city and will see a man with the water pitcher, and go into the house of the man with the water pitcher. That is the house of Aquarius. There is an encoded message in the New Testament, almost all of it was written in an allegorical sense. That's why Jesus said, "Many will look with their eyes, but not see. And they will listen with their ears, but not hear. " Many have read the Bible and listened to sermons in churches for thousands of years, and they have looked with their eyes, but did not see. And they have listened to sermons with their ears, but did not hear.

PT: So the fundamentalist Christians are the furthest from the truth when they think they have the whole truth. Is that what you are saying?

JM: Well, there's a scripture where Jesus said, "If you say that you are in the light, but in fact you are in the dark, then how dark your light really is." The point made is if you think you have the whole truth and the correct understanding, you had better make sure you do. Because if you don't, you are really in the dark. And my point on this is that humility is required to understand spiritual things. We need to be humble enough to admit that we might not have read the scriptures correctly.

PT: Your career is starting to take off, and you are getting noticed everywhere. How do you think the church will perceive you? And the public in general?

JM: There's no doubt that many in the church, no matter what denomination, will perceive me as an antichrist or at least working on the side of an antichrist. But it has also been my experience in talking to thousands of people, lecturing in auditoriums and before various groups where many of these people were church-going Christians. And I've found the majority of them were favorably disposed toward me and what I am saying. They do not show themselves to be hostile at all, and seem to be impressed with the things that they're learning. The people who will see me as being on the side of an antichrist will be those who have something to lose. Those who have a vested interest, who are employed and might lose their employment. And people who are sincerely searching for knowledge and truth never shy away from challenges to learn. And something I have learned is that truth can stand on its own, and never needs to be validated by ignorance and bigotry. As Gerald Massey wrote, "They must find it difficult, those who have accepted the authority as the truth, rather than truth as the authority." Those who have accepted our government and church authority as being correct are going to find that when you are faced with spiritual truth, this truth has nothing in common with those authorities.

PT: Does this mean you know what that spiritual truth is? Are you hinting at having a monopoly on the truth, as many religions claim?

JM: I believe that I am on my own path to truth, and with a similar understanding, many others might find their own paths easier. In the Indiana Jones movie "The Last Crusade," Indiana Jones is saying to his class that if you are looking for truth, then you are in the wrong class. Truth is found in the philosophy and religion department, that's where truth is found. "As an archaeologist," he said, "I am concerned with facts, not truth." And the reason why, is that all educated people know that truth is subjective. Things that are true to you, may not be true to me.

PT: That's true.

JM: That's why in a court of law, we're not looking for someone to tell "the truth," we're looking for what can be proven by facts. Whether you tell the truth or not. If you have preconceived ideas, that is a very bad starting point. How would you like to be on trial, for your life and have the 12 jurors already decided on your case?

PT: So you would want people to approach you in the same way – with an open mind.

JM: Right. At least hear what I have to say before you make a judgment. I could be wrong. And that's what I've always said. I could be wrong.

PT: But if you're right...

JM: But if I'm right, it means that the whole authoritarian system that we see around us is wrong, and it has usurped the position of our Creator. The governments and churches both have usurped the great spiritual God-force that exists and that we have a right to. The American Indians referred to it as "The Great Spirit," and most of the ancient peoples of the world recognized it. That is what man owes his first and only allegiance to – that great creative force in the universe that gave us life and gives you freedom.

PT: That reminds me of the Chief Seattle speech that was reprinted in the book that you also appeared in *The Book Your Church Doesn't Want You To Read*. He said that we all have the same God.

JM: And that's exactly right. But today, in the Western world in particular, we have given ourselves – our bodies, our minds, and our money – over to politics, to government, and to churches, instead of to that Great Spirit. That makes a very big connection between church and government. They share this same "territory." And now, we are finally seeing the outcome of all this chicanery. America, one of the greatest countries ever on the face of the Earth is now on its knees because so many of its people are broke, and serving "other masters."

PT: We're also deep in debt as a country.

JM: True. And no matter which side of the political spectrum it's from, everyone perceives that America is in serious, serious trouble. It is no longer something to talk about, it is something you had better worry about. Because if this country goes under and a "New World Order" comes in, then so goes freedom, liberty, and spiritual and intellectual enlightenment for the whole world, I believe. It's time for all people who love truth to stand up and acknowledge that organized religion and government have failed. They are not leaders. They are misleaders. They have purposely misled us. And I believe that there is a higher spiritual force in this universe that is going to deal with this state, with this government, and with this religion, and with us if we continue to be a part of it.

PT: You have said that religion and government have failed. That reminds me of two quotes from *The Book Your Church Doesn't Want You To Read*. Pertaining to religion Robert Ingersoll said, "Religion can never reform mankind because religion is slavery." And on politics, James Madison once said, "I believe there are more instances of the abridgement of the freedom of the people by gradual and silent encroachments of those in power than by violent and sudden usurpations."

JM: That's exactly how the ones at the top are doing it, taking our freedoms. It's the old story of the frog put into the pan of cold water, then the fire put under him slowly. The water becomes hot gradually, so that the frog doesn't notice that he's being cooked until it's too late – then it dawns on him that he's been had.

PT: Otherwise, if you'd have put the heat up right away...

JM: ...then he'd have felt it right away, and would never have bought into it. Americans today would never have bought into what is happening today in this country 50 years ago. People 50 years ago would turn in their graves if they could see what has happened to their beloved country.

PT: So what would happen, hypothetically, then, if indeed this country did go down the tubes, if our debts were completely out of control and somebody had to come in with an iron fist and rule over us?

JM: That's precisely what will happen, if we're not very, very careful. Another Adolf Hitler is about to be born.

PT: So what can we do to avert that, if you can see that happening on the horizon? We want to have some hope here.

JM: I believe it's very likely that the same kind of tyranny experienced in Nazi Germany is on the way for America. The first thing we have to do is awaken ourselves spiritually enough to understand that we owe our thoughts, our decisions, and our lives to our higher, spiritual selves and to the spiritual power in the universe that created us – and not to our churches, reverends, preachers, not to government, not to bureaucrats, not to any human being on this Earth that puts their clothes on the same way you do. They are not in any more position of spiritual authority than any one else. That's the first thing we have to do, because right now we are not only getting poorer financially, we are very poor intellectually and spiritually.

PT: So you're saying that this spiritual ignorance, this drought that we're in now – that our deepest problems are the result of that.

JM: That's exactly what I'm saying. The problems that we face throughout the world are spiritual problems, and not political. If we were spiritually awake and spiritually alert and alive, we would never, ever allow the kinds of things that are happening in this country and in the world. But one thing our "masters" in this country know, as all tyrants have always known, is if they can get you to sell out your morality, your ethics, and your scruples for money, pleasure and money, then you will no longer be a threat or be able to defend your freedom. Because you are then dependent on their alcohol, their money, their drugs, their motion pictures, entertainments, and various other diversions. You become so jaded in your materialistic lust for everything just mentioned, that you will just be quiet as long as you can have what makes you happy. Once you have your porno films, alcohol, or whatever keeps you quiet, you will never stand up to those who provide it unless you are morally, ethically, and in every other way prepared to stand on your own, by yourself, and not be a slave to anyone.

PT: Why is it that you have said that the church is in no position to represent the highest spiritual authority? I'm wondering, is that because they can't make you realize your spiritual potential for you, but that you've got to do it yourself?

JM: Yes, that is one consideration. They cannot make you a spiritual person.

But I would take that a step further by saying that the organized church today, in the Western world, beginning with the Roman Catholic Church in the year 325, needs to be studied very closely. The scriptural precedent was set by the words of Jesus, who once said, "Can a bad tree give forth good fruit?" I'd say that's impossible. So if that is true, then Protestants, who protested against Rome and set up their own organizational church, became an offspring, so to speak. And if Catholicism is the bad tree, then according to a quote from their theology, Protestants are equally as bad, since a bad tree cannot give forth good fruit. What I'm saying is that religion in the western world, as we know it, is nothing more than a political movement. An entirely bad tree that took more than 300 years to organize because of scheming and in-fighting. It was organized and later directed from "behind the scenes," as it still is today. Martin Luther, for example, was influenced by sinister people, some who were Freemasons, for purely political reasons – to divide the power of the church. And when you see the church in this context, as a political movement continually playing a part in the bigger picture, then you can understand why religion and government are one and the same.

PT: You quote from the Bible often. How do you view the Bible?

JM: The entire story of the New Testament is an astrological story. That's interesting, since we have been told not to have anything to do with fortune-telling or astrology. And yet, in Genesis, Amos 5:8, and the Book of Job, Job 37:18, and Job 9:9, the Bible very clearly talks about how God created the heavens, or zodiac. And in Job 38:32 God asks, "Can you direct the signs of the zodiac, or guide the constellation of the bear?" This includes the proper translation of the word "Mazzaroth" into "zodiac," used in Moffatt's English Bible and The New English Bible, for example. Yet, many other versions don't bother to translate the word, but leave it as "Mazzaroth," to the confusion of all readers (as in King James). And the entire scriptures are filled with the idea that God created the 12 signs of the zodiac. That's why Jesus is called "the son," God's SUN, who has 12 helpers, or the 12 signs of the zodiac. And in the very beginning, Genesis 1 :14, the scripture says God created the luminaries of the night – the stars – for *signs*. We're talking about zodialogical signs. We have a misunderstanding as to what the scriptures are saying, overall, and we need to get past the misunderstandings that we have been led into by the churches.

PT: Who was it in the Bible, was it Saul, who denounced witches? The Bible says he banished them from the land. Then four verses later he says, "Bring me a witch! "

JM: Yes, King Saul. What is interesting about that is all of Christianity says that when Saul went to the witch of Endor to bring up Samuel, he went to this witch and asked her to contact the prophet Samuel, who was dead, and the witch did that. Christianity said, "Well, that wasn't really Samuel, it was a demon who made himself appear to be Samuel." But the fact is, if you read the account, in One Samuel, it says "And the witch brought up Samuel and Samuel talked to...," and it does not say it was a demon or a spirit that was acting like Samuel, it was Samuel.

PT: So there's a contradiction there. I've heard many contradictions are also found in the four main New Testament Gospels.

JM: Yes, it's there if you look. And there is additional information being kept from us or covered up. This is a direct quote, if you wish to quote me: I am saying that the most heinous criminals that have ever existed in this world, from what I can tell by a study of history, are here today, in America. Leading this country, as politicians on a state level, and especially on the federal level, are the most heinous criminals the world has ever known. These men are not politicians and leaders, they are misleaders, they are criminals. They have caused this country to be sold out to its enemies, they have bled us dry, our finances, they have stolen from us, and we are now in the same footsteps the Roman empire was in the early fourth century, just before the total collapse of the empire. America has been in decline for the past 30 to 40 years for sure. We are heading for a total decline and ultimate collapse. Somewhere along the line the people are going to wake up and find out their churches have not told them this. The churches have purposely kept the people sleeping, and depending on "The Lord who is to come," and looking for tomorrow, and don't worry about today, don't put up any resistance, just do whatever the government says, and have faith in God.

PT: Isn't this church mentality a repeating pattern in history?

JM: Over and over. When we came out of the Dark Ages into the Age of Enlightenment, the leaders of The Enlightenment were eventually put to death by the church. And the church always put to death anyone who would go against church or government. I believe the two greatest enemies of all free people in the world are government and religion, both. They are both equal partners in tyranny and have sold us out. The government fleeces us, the church fleeces us. That's why Christians are called sheep. Because with sheep, you fleece them. And then you eat them. And sheep, of course, are the dumbest animals in the world, and any farmer will tell you that. It's true. Anyone who knows anything about animals and animal husbandry will tell you that the most incredibly stupidest animal the world has ever known is a sheep. They cannot find their way out of a paper bag, and they will follow anybody.

PT: So what you're saying is, "Wake up, and don't be eaten."

JM: Right. Somewhere along the line, we've got to take back not only our country, but our spirituality.

PT: So you are saying that we need to take back our spirituality and our country from a powerful, shadowy movement that is slowly encroaching on us. How can we do that?

JM: As I've said, we need to wake up, first, because people don't even know we've lost these things. To stay asleep, all you have to do as an American is what you've always done – nothing. All your masters have to do is what they've always done and sooner or later, their timetable for taking you over, completely destroying your freedom, your country, your spirituality, will have come and their goal will be accomplished.

PT: So we need to wake up first. In *The Book Your Church Doesn't Want You to Read*, it mentions Joan of Arc, saying after her church and country had totally discredited her, then killed her by burning her alive, the church turned around 500 years later and made her a saint. They did not accept her contribution until later.

JM: This church, government, and the forces behind it are acting in the same way today and won't see their mistakes until later. They are the enemy of not only humans, but of God. I suppose we are doomed to repeat history until we get it right.

PT: You spoke about forces "behind the scenes." What is going on behind the scenes that we are now all up against?

JM: We are in the hands of very powerful Secret Societies and Fraternal Orders that are bent on having complete power over us and the world as a whole. This goal involves the destruction of America's way of life, our way of thinking, and our freedom. Our government is being manipulated by something higher – that is why I've said we've been "sold out." Government was set up in this country to do one thing – that is, to do for the people, generally, that which they can't do for themselves. This means, more specifically, to provide for our protection as a nation, to provide for an orderly distribution of goods, and for law and order. That's all. Not coming into your bedroom, telling you what you can think, or read, or say on the radio, where you can go, what health foods or vitamins you can buy, where your kids go to school, what medications you can get, all of these things are part of a tyrannical control system that is seeping into our lives. Our government and America in general is definitely – and it could be proven in a court of law – definitely in the hands of Secret Societies and Fraternal Orders that trace back to the Middle Ages –

Knighthoods, for example, The Knights Templars. And this is where banking, and money, comes in. When you go into a bank today and do any kind of transaction, borrowing money, using a checking account, anything, it was all started around the year 900 when banks began on an international basis. This was started by an organization called "The Order of the Knights of the Temple of Solomon," or "The Order of Knights Templar." And today, all banking is in the hands of Knights Templars Masonic Orders, Freemasons. One of the concordant orders of Freemasonry was called "The Knights of the Order of the Hospital," and they were called "Knights Hospitalers." They were the Masonic Order that founded, organizes, directs, and finances Hospitals and health care, throughout the world. That is why you'll see hospitals using various Masonic symbols or emblems, if you look closely enough. So these same people, overall, control banking, hospitals, and even the entertainment we see. They finance and organize your media, so you will know only what they want you to know.

PT: There's a lot more of that than people realize.

JM: Absolutely. And you know, Merlin and the old magicians of Celtic England always used their magic wands, and these magic wands were always made out of holly wood. And that's why today we still have Holly-wood, working its "magic" on us – showing us in movies how to view things, what we should think, or just offering us a big box office diversion. Hollywood is in California, but the money and the brains are on the east coast, among maybe four or five families, that control almost all of Hollywood from New York. So we're talking about some very powerful families, that are left unnamed, who own and operate almost all of Hollywood. All major media entertainment companies have their corporate offices in New York, and that is not just coincidence.

PT: Do you feel that our country has been deliberately sold out because there is kind of a conspiracy going on for a one-world government?

JM: Oh, there's no doubt in my mind about that. I think even the most ignorant people today, the most ill-informed, pretty well have figured that out. I think it's pretty obvious.

PT: So banks and money have a strong hand in that?

JM: They don't have a hand in it, they are the culprits. The international monetary system, set up earlier by The Knights Templar, have in mind the total eradication of freedom, and liberty, across the whole world. And if America goes down, all freedom and liberty in the world will go down with it. America is the last stronghold on the Earth for the opportunity to be free. These Secret Societies (including The Knights Templars and Knights Hospitalers) are feverishly working behind the scenes to destroy our morals, our ethics, and our country, and to ultimately bring about a "New World Order" – "Novus Ordo Seclorum," which is of course found on the back of a dollar bill. What's interesting in relation to that is the pyramid on the back of the dollar. Jesus is twice referred in the New Testament as the "chief cornerstone that the builders rejected." The apostles were referred to as cornerstones, but "chief cornerstone" in Greek is different from "cornerstone," and that is how Jesus was referred. The chief cornerstone is the triangle that sits on top of a pyramid. And in the Book of Isaiah 19:19, God says, "I will have a temple and an altar in the midst of the land of Egypt" (It is a "temple and pillar" in the King James Bible). That "temple and altar" is one thing, not two, because the scripture goes on to say, "And it shall be as a symbol and an emblem for God in the land of Egypt." What we're talking about, this "it," is the Great Pyramid in Egypt because the pyramid does sit directly in the midst of Egypt, on the border between upper and lower Egypt. So the pyramid, according to the Bible, Isaiah 19:19, was put there by God – it was God's will that that pyramid be there. Second, Jesus is referred to as "the chief cornerstone," which means, in Greek, "the peak of a pyramid." What I'm saying is there's a profound depth to the symbolism on a dollar bill, and the words. An additional phrase on it, above the pyramid, is "Annuit Coeptis," meaning "Our enterprise has been crowned with success." This project or enterprise is The New Order of the World – "Novus Ordo Seclorum" – printed directly beneath it. This is an example of the tremendous amount of esoteric knowledge that has been kept from us. It is time that we turn off the television and the basketball, the football, the volleyball, the ping pong ball, and all the other ball games, and step back from the alcohol, all the entertainments, and look seriously at who we are and where we're going because wherever it is that we're going (and it doesn't look good), we're gonna get there real quick. This country is in serious trouble, but people are being told that everything is fine.

PT: Well, when people are suddenly deprived of all of their diversions, then they'll finally get the message – we've been had. But are people that blind, not to see it beforehand?

JM: Not blind, just bigoted. The old saying was that "When they came to kill Catholics I didn't bother because I wasn't a Catholic. And when they came to take away the Jews, I didn't say anything because I wasn't a Jew. And when they came to take away Protestants I wasn't a Protestant, so by the time they came for me, there was no one else left to help, and to protect me. " The point is, we should put aside all the bigotry, prejudice, and stupidity. In this country, we are all one people, and should act that way. We need to realize that we all face the same danger. Look at the leaders in America, the ones who are supposedly spokesmen for the people. In every case you will always find that these officials do not speak for the good of the people they represent, they are out there for themselves, only.

PT: The lobbyists are just paying them off, and they do what they're told to do.

JM: That's exactly right. So somewhere along the line, we have to come together as one people, without the corrupted "help" of the politicians. Or the church. Those who can see this happening, and are willing to act, I believe have a cosmic companionship. Martin Luther King said it best. He said, "In this struggle, we will be successful because we have cosmic companionship." I am totally convinced that that is precisely the case here. People who are standing up now, in this time, for freedom and for human dignity, do have a cosmic companionship with the Creator that gave us life. And I think somewhere along the line, the enemies are going to be exposed. No lie can live forever. Plato once said that, "The price good people pay for non-involvement in public affairs is to be ruled by evil men." There has never been a time that we have been ruled by evil men, if not today. And they work not only out in front, and recognized, but also from behind the scenes, in secret. Yet, this government has a very powerful enemy that it is frightened to death of. It is not Russia, or the return of Naziism, or middle eastern fanatics. The most dangerous enemy that the United States government is facing today, and it knows it, is you. You as a spiritual individual with your own rights, freedoms, and liberties to be your own self and do your own thinking. Because these things are being slowly eroded away, in hopes that we won't notice.

PT: Our educational system is also being eroded. Much lower SAT's, kids don't know many simple geographical facts, the list goes on and on. Do you think there's an intentional "dumbing down" of our society taking place?

JM: I sure do. The powers that be are keeping us docile with endless diversions – movies, television, entertainments like mindless Nintendo and computer games, drugs, alcohol, they hand out condoms in some schools. And when you get kids while they're young, they develop bad learning habits and short attention spans. A ton of information has also surfaced connecting certain intelligence agencies with the drug trade into America. And who does drugs? Mostly young people. There's no doubt about an intentional dumbing down, you can't possibly get around that. And when these people grow up, as a generation, nobody will be smart enough to know what to stand up for. Just think about the "Little House on the Prairie" days, back in the 1800's and early 1900's, when the schoolrooms were one little schoolroom out in the middle of the prairie with all the different grades sitting together.

And out of these meager beginnings, out of these schoolhouses, came the great captains and kings of industry, the great poets, the great mathematicians, the greatest minds that built America and made it the strongest and most profoundly important country in the world. And today, we have the greatest schools, with air conditioning and all the computers and, collectively, they can't find their way home. They are the most ignorant and ill-informed generation this country has ever produced. It's been said that 50 per cent of high school graduates can't find America on an unlabeled world map. Now that's frightening.

PT: The NEA, the National Education Association, could be held largely responsible. It is among the four most powerful associations in the country. It funds the education in America, controls the labor, and is said to be more of a political group (instead of a union), concerned with only power and money – not education. Dr. William Coulson helped found it about 30 years ago, but totally renounces it today because of its "Values Modification" agenda. This new agenda seems directly linked to the growth of drug use and sexual misconduct by young people. The NEA's spending has increased more than 300 per cent since 1960, but student performance has plummeted. The NEA controls virtually all public education in America today, but doesn't seem to care about the kids. People say it's power and money they want. An obvious tie-in to the conspiracy against America?

JM: Absolutely. Our children are being systematically reconditioned into stupidity. And it's working. The kids don't seem like they want to learn.

PT: They'd rather go home and watch MTV.

JM: Yes, or Big Top Pee-Wee or Hulk Hogan. So what we're faced with is a very serious collapse of Western civilization. And no one wants to admit it. And consequently, like all other ancient empires have found out, there comes a time of reckoning. Our country is going the same route as the fall of Rome, and if it happens, the world stands a chance of being cast into another Dark Ages.

PT: But aren't there forces within our government that are really on our side? I remember a very reliable source from within our government who went by the name of "Mr. Mike." You spent a day with him once. He detailed how there were two factions behind the scenes in our government, one working for a way to salvage or preserve our freedoms, and the other on working to accomplish the kind of world dominance you've detailed.

JM: Yes, I'm aware that there are others who are awake and aware, and who are allying themselves with each other to do something. I don't know who those organizations might be, but I do know from my travels around the country that many of the average people I lecture to know that what I am saying is true, on a semi-grass roots level, and they understand the seriousness of the problems we are facing. And I am sure that this government is absolutely frightened to death that these people will turn off the television and get organized. And that's the one thing they cannot afford to allow to happen.

PT: Not only getting organized, but educated.

JM: Yes, that's the most dangerous thing you can do – educate people. Because when people become educated, you cannot control them, you cannot frighten them. People who are educated know their own power, and don't surrender it to others. I prefer to die someday on my feet, rather than on my knees. An idea who's time has come is individuality and freedom, and understanding that both religion and government in America are the enemies of all good people. All sincerely decent, good people have as their greatest enemy this government and the people behind this government who are manipulating it, and the churches, period!

PT: What would you say to the people who are the real patriotic types who would tell you, "America, love it or leave it. Why don't you just get the hell out if you think the government and churches are the enemy?"

JM: They must have said about the same thing in Rome, about the fourth century, when everything was falling apart. I'm sure there were many people who said, "Well, it's still Rome, it's still the greatest and most powerful place in the world," and I hear people saying that today about America.

PT: Didn't Nero play the fiddle while Rome was burning?

JM: Yeah, well, he might as well have played the fiddle. If he didn't, he should have. We're playing the fiddle right now – I think that was a symbolic story. I don't think Nero ever played a fiddle to start with. It means that while the entire Roman empire was collapsing from the weight of its own filth and corruption, the emperor did nothing. The president of our country does nothing; he does nothing because he can do nothing. He is nothing more than the slave of a slave state, the powers that be, behind his "throne" are the masters of this country. He is just a symbol and a figurehead who has as much power as you do. Actually, he has less power. And what you have to remember is that the president of America is not your president, legally. The United States federal government is a foreign corporation. According to international maritime admiralty law, the federal government of America is a foreign corporation, in respect to the states. It is a total, separate unit of power in this country, it has nothing whatsoever to do with the separate states. It is a corporation, founded under international corporate law. And corporate law says that all corporations must have a president and a vice president. The federal government in DC is nothing more than a business. All the wars we've ever fought were nothing more than hostile takeovers (or attempts at such) by very powerful monetary figures working behind the scenes, using this corporation called the federal government of the United States. It's nothing but a company, and a war is nothing but a hostile takeover.

PT: So can we look at this and say we have just contracted out the services of this corporation to run our country?

JM: That's exactly right. So when you accept a social security card or other federal I.D., what you have done is you've made yourself a franchise. You are then a member of the federal corporation, living in a separate state, and are legally a franchisee of the federal system in Washington, DC. That's why when you pay taxes for the state of California you pay the Franchise Tax Board. When you get your bill at the end of the year for your federal taxes, write out a check and send the check to "The U.S. Dept. of the Treasury." And they will send it back to you with a form letter, telling you that you do not owe the Treasury of the United States anything. You owe this money to The Federal Reserve Corporation. It is a private corporation. Your federal taxes do not go to pay government in this country, they go to the corporation just mentioned. The federal tax system came into existence in 1934-35. America became the most powerful monetary nation on Earth from 1776 to 1935 without a federal income tax, without a state income tax, without any income tax.

PT: Is that when the gold standard was done away with?

JM: That's right. Incidentally, that's precisely the year that those symbols and slogans were put there on the back of the dollar bill. Because once they got the Federal Reserve into position, locked into position illegally, but locked into a position of power, then they could put on the dollar "Annuit Coeptis," "Our Enterprise is now a Success," meaning, "We have now taken over America, and America was sound asleep and didn't even know it." So what I'm saying is that we have all been had. We've been had politically, and religiously. Until such time that we wake up, we are headed toward total and complete disaster. I hate to end on such a down note, but those are the facts and we need to wake up.

PT: Jordan, I'd like to end by giving you a quote from Thomas Merton, who was a Roman Catholic monk. He said, "The most dangerous man in the world is the contemplative who is guided by nobody. He trusts his own visions. He obeys the attractions of an inner voice, but will not listen to other men. He identifies the will of God with his own heart." Jordan Maxwell, you are a dangerous man.

JM: Thank you.

Hello, I'm Jordan Maxwell, this is a transcript from two separate interviews that were conducted not too long ago. The woman who interviewed me was Rita Dyson the man was Ralph Walker. The response to these interviews when they first aired was so overwhelming that we wanted to include them in this book.

> *Of all the tyrannies that affect mankind, tyranny in religion is the worst. Every other species of tyranny is limited to the world we live in, but religion attempts to strive beyond the grave and seeks to pur - sue us into eternity.*
>
> —Thomas Paine

RD: Jordan, you've got to tell me about yourself.

JM: Well, my grandfather was a senator, my great-grandfather was a congress-man, I have two living uncles that are federal judges, so I grew up hearing this kind of conversation in the family, about intrigue and politics, and the behind the scenes stuff going on in world religion. At the ripe old age of 17 I decided that I wanted to find out if there was a bottom to this issue and I began my research and study into theology and all of the arcane and occult theologies. I was fascinated by some of the most powerful movements in the world.But the problem you run into with reli-gion and theology is that there are two kinds of facts that we have in theology, the kind you look up and the kind you make up. And so much of what we've been told and led to believe in theology and religion, especially in the western world, is noth-ing more than political propaganda. Over and above the political aspect of western religion, I'm also fascinated with the general anthology of religion. By anthology I mean things that most people would not know about religion, things the church would rather you not know. For instance, one of my favorite topics is called astro-theology, which is the world's oldest religion and dates back to 5,000 to 7,000 years before Christ. At that time, the worship of the heavens dominated the world. I don't believe there are too many people today in our western civilization that have real-ly looked at where their religion, their ideas, and concepts, really come from. We are all aware of how other people can be wrong in what they believe. We have a theology and other people have a mythology. According to our own narrow, per-sonal viewpoints, other people are wrong because they don't share our concepts and beliefs, and that's because they don't understand. They're wrong, but they don't understand.

I am saying that we can all be wrong. There is not one human crea-ture on the earth that is so well-informed that they could possibly not be wrong about some-thing. All I'm asking my audience to do is to look at the facts of where western religion has come from, and look at the behind-the-scenes connections between government

The judge sits three tiers high and wears a black robe, representing the first three degrees of Freemasonry and the color of the planet-god, Saturn.

and religion. Let me give you a quick example between tying government and religion together. When you go into most churches today you'll see that the altar is three tiers high, it's three degrees high. In most churches they have a fence and a gate and only the priest can go through the gate up onto the altar. When the priest comes out he's dressed in a long robe and everyone stands out of respect. It's the same as in any courtroom, when they say "all rise," when the judge comes out. You have the people of the congregation out in the courtroom, you have the fence and the gate, and only the attorneys can go through and speak for you. And the bench is three tiers high, the three tiers high in both the church and the courtroom represent the first three degrees of freemasonry. When the judge comes out he's dressed in a long black robe, just as the priest is dressed in a long black robe, just as you will be dressed in a long robe when you graduate from a university or college. The connections are continual. The judge can sit and look down on you, and represents the law, spelled L-A-W. You need to look at where the "law" comes from. And then of course, the priest can look down on the audience – and to the people in the church he represents God, which is the law.

RD: So you're saying that people should start looking at things with a different eye that what they're used to. People just take it for granted that this has always been, and this is the way it is.

JM: Absolutely.

RD: But there is an origin for every one of these things.

JM: Gerald Massey, one of the greatest Egyptologists that ever lived, wrote that "They will find it difficult, those who have accepted the authority as truth, rather than the truth as authority." So, I'm saying that that's what's happened to us as a civilization in the West. I'm not interested that much in the East tonight. I'm interested in our western way of life; the religion, the philosophies that guide our lives, the mere fact that in this country in America when you run afoul of the law, you have broken the law, just as Moses broke the law. It goes back to Judaism. And of course the sheriff has the six-pointed badge, which represents the Star of David, or the six-pointed hexagram. All of our judicial proceedings in court are based on the old common law of England, or Britannia. It's a fascinating story once people understand that our government is based on religion and we didn't even know it.

RD: Okay. You have such a vast amount of information that I have to try and hold you back a minute, because I want to get to other information.

JM: Okay.

RD: Let me ask this. How would you classify yourself? Are you religious, are you spiritual, are you agnostic, what are you?

JM: I am a common man, an ordinary man; in the pursuit of an extraordinary subject. I consider myself to be one who appreciates and will fight for truth.

The university graduate wears the black robe of the god Saturn and the mortarboard of Freemasonry. Both are very ancient symbols.

RD: You are a truthseeker?

JM: I think that's probably the best way to term it. I am an extremely spiritual person in that I hold very high spiritual morals and ethics. I believe in a very powerful spiritual force that dominates and overshadows this world. Christians call it God, others may call it something else. I have a very high respect for spirituality. I have no time for religion as such. Anything that is organized by man, quite certainly is not touching god. I think that we have a direct connection with our creator, that great spiritual God-force, we don't need another man to intervene for us.

RD: Okay, let's say that someone may say "How dare you question the Bible. How dare you speak like this, you must be a demon or something." How would you answer that?

JM: I would say the same thing has been said of Solomon Rushdie, "How dare you question The Koran. How dare you question Karl Marx and the Communist Manifesto. Or Mao and the Little Red Book of Mao. How dare you question authority!" I'm saying that the man we read about in the New Testament, the one called Jesus, if he taught us anything, it was to question authority. Any time you give away your spirituality and your authority, and you do it yourself, you know, no one comes and puts your hands behind your back, and forces to give up you spirituality and your individual freedom, and your right to be a human being and decide for yourself; you do that yourself. And when you do that, and you give up your sovereignty to the government, to the church, to a religion, to a book, to a concept, to anything, you are enslaving yourself. All I'm asking the public to do is to do a little research, see if what I'm saying is wrong, and judge for yourself. I'm not advocating anything or running for any political office, and I'm not trying to start my own church. What I would like to see happen is a spiritual revolution in this country, where people say "just say no," just say no to organized religion, just say no to organized government, just say no to tyranny. I don't care where it is, or what color it is, just say no to bigotry, ignorance, ill-informed stupidity, just say no, from here on out.

RD: But if…

JM: The point I'm making is that you need to do your homework. You need to study and find out where things came from.

RD: But what happens when they do find out? What happens to those whose whole life has been the Bible? There's so many people that are kept going every day by the Bible. What will they have to replace it?

JM: Ask the Russians, in Russia today, what is it like when you find out you've been hood-winked, that your government was not the most powerful or the most wonderful government on earth and now it has totally collapsed? What do you do now? You trusted, you brought up your children, you wasted your entire life, and you went along to get along. And now what happens? Your entire world is collapsing around you, and why? Because you didn't do your homework, and you didn't stand up for what was right when you could have. You went along to get along, because it was comfortable at the time, and now it's very uncomfortable. And I'm saying that's what we all have to do is look at the uncomfortable fact that nothing is permanently on this earth.

RD: That nothing is permanently on this earth.

JM: That's right. Things constantly change. The Russians should have seen it coming, and who was really controlling them. Maybe we can learn something from what Russia has experienced. In 1922 Winston Churchill spoke to the London Press and said, "From the days of Sparticus, Wieskhopf, Karl Marx, Trotsky, Rosa Luxemberg, and Emma Goldman, this world conspiracy has been steadily growing. This conspiracy played a definite recognizable role in the tragedy of the French revolution. It has been the mainspring of every subversive movement during the

19th century. And now at last, this band of extraordinary personalities from the underworld of the great cities of Europe and America have gripped the Russian people by the hair of their head and have become the undisputed masters of that enormous empire." And look at where those "masters" brought them –. into chaos, and now leading them into what is hoped to be The New World Order. That's why the Soviet Union collapsed. In the Washington Post (May 1991) Brent Scowcroft announced that "We believe we are creating the beginning of a New World Order coming out of the collapse of the U.S.-Soviet antagonisms." What I'm saying is that it was planned, and a one world government could never function before that.

RD: That's amazing. On another subject, in the book you were part of, *The Book Your Church Doesn't Want You to Read*, they have here Bible models, Bible morality. And this was Thomas Jefferson that wrote this. Who was Jehovah? A being of terrific character, cruel, vindictive, capricious, and unjust. And then also, who was Abraham? An insane barbarian patriarch, who married his sister and denied his wife. Who was Jacob? Another patriarch who won God's favor by deceiving his father, cheating his uncle, and robbing his brother. This is Bible morality.

JM: Now understand, I didn't write that. Other authors have contributed to the book. But the point I wish to make is that one does not even need to read the book.

RD: Okay.

JM: One can just read the Bible and put flesh on things that happened in the Bible. Think about it.

RD: What I just mentioned is in the Bible?

JM: Of course it is. Now let me ask you something. Are you aware that there were fifteen other major religions, this is history now...

RD: Okay.

JM: ...not conjecture, history. There were fifteen major theological religious movements before Christianity that taught the same identical story. Of a messiah who came to the earth, who was born in a manger, who died on a cross, who had twelve apostles, who died with a crown of thorns. Were you aware that there were fifteen major religions that had the same identical teachings of Christianity? Most people aren't. And I'm very suspect of a sixteenth religion which is copied off of fifteen previous religions, and I am told that this one is the truth. I become very suspect. That is the way I am as a teacher and as a researcher and writer. And I tell you something else I'm very suspect of and that is the connection between government and politics today in America. I think both should be investigated. We need to look behind the scenes of our authorities in the world – of religion, politics, and money.

RD: When that happens, people will have a renaissance for themselves.

JM: Let us hope so.

RD: And a whole new type of person can come about.

JM: I think you will agree that that's what we need. Our country is in trouble, our families are in trouble, our whole human race is in trouble. Basically we can boil it down to three problems that we all share on this earth; religion, politics, and money. And I'm telling you that the three are not separate, they are all one, because in the ancient world the king always represented not only temple power, but also heavenly power, he was the connection between the people and God. That is why you can not get married today without a blessing of the government, and in many cases the church. We are told there is a division between church and state. No such division exists. If you want to start a church you must get a 501c3 permit from the government, you must get permits, you must pay the fees, you must do all of these legal things, go through the red tape of the government, before you can set up a church. Now, in this church, with all the government's permission and permits, you can not get married in this country unless you have a license first, from the state. Then you can go to the minister and be married. And then, if your marriage doesn't work out, you don't go to God, you go to a judge, in a courtroom. I'm telling you there's something going on here between religion and politics, and it's money, it's power. We need to be willing to look at what's been going on in this country for over 200 years, and be open minding about it. Remember, your mind is a like a parachute, it will not work if it's not open. We can be exploited if we're not willing to open our minds and open our hearts and say, "let's look at the facts." The fact is that all over the world people are being led by religious leaders. Ayatolah Khomeini and Saddam Hussein are just two of many religious leaders that have been fanatically dangerous. And in this country we had put things on the backs of our cars, and yellow ribbons in our trees, to fanatically support our troops in the Middle East, when we didn't even know what they were really doing there.

RD: Do you think religion and politics has something to do with this New World Order, this global unification we've heard so much about?

JM: That you can bet on.

RD: You do?

JM: I think I could make a very good case for that in a court of law, if given the opportunity. Let's look at the symbolism going on here. Like the Washington Monument in Washington, DC. The Washington Monument is an Egyptian obelisk, which stands for the male erection. That is its original symbolism. It connects right down to "the waters of life" that you see at its base, over to the oval office. The oval is the female, the Washington Monument is the male. It has to do with religion, it has to do with sex, it has to do with political power. And we take these instruments, and we take these symbols, and we think they are so marvelous. Do your homework and you'll find out that so much of what we consider to be holy and righteous is nothing more than sex, religion, and money. And most people pretty much know that, but no one has bothered to confront the establishment. I hope to do that. I want to confront the establishment because I believe that the truth is an idea whose time has come. I think we've all been manipulated and exploited and it's time we looked at the real truth.

RD: I think that a lot of people are walking around in a daze. There are so many things happening that they don't know where to turn.

JM: Absolutely.

RD: And I think that many of them don't feel really happy with what they are receiving in church, when they do go to church.

JM: Absolutely.

RD: They feel something is wrong.

JM: It's because something *is* wrong. The things which we have been told are not true. You can prove this in any good library. All one has to do is go to the library and spend all day there, reading theology, and you will find that the world has known for thousands of years that these stories are nothing more than stories. As a matter of fact, Rita, the Bible is called the greatest story ever told. The greatest story, not the greatest collection of facts, not the most paramount document on Earth, it's the greatest story ever told. It's a story. One must know how to read the symbols and the emblems, and the terms.

RD: The symbols are in the Bible too?

JM: The symbols are in the Bible everywhere. Did you know, for instance, that the Book of Revelation was not written by Christians? The Book of Revelation was around for at least 500 years before Christianity ever came into existence. The Book of Revelation was already in circulation, therefore no John ever wrote the Book of Revelation. His name was Ion, from the Ionian Sea, but when translating from Latin, when you change the letter "I" to "J" it becomes J-o-n, or Jon.

However, when you translate it to English, J-o-n becomes J-o-h-n, or John. So today we're told that John wrote the Book of Revelation. No such John ever wrote the Book of Revelation. It was written long before Christ was ever born.

RD: This is just earthshaking.

JM: Wait until the real truth comes out about religion and politics in America and you're going to see the earth shake.

RD: Are you ready for the tomatoes? Are you ready for that?

JM: I've already gotten those many times.

RD: Okay. Now in the book *The Book Your Church Doesn't Want You to Read*, you have an article entitled Astro-theology.

JM: Yes. I co-edited the book with Tim Leedom, but also did a chapter on astro-theology.

RD: And I wanted to mention Steve Allen, the famous entertainer and former Tonight Show host, who also wrote in this book.

JM: Yes, Steve Allen is a brilliant writer and is a part of our book. He and I became friends since the book's release.

RD: We opened up with that quote from Thomas Paine. You must like Thomas Paine because you also quote him in your writing.

JM: Yes, I think he was an absolutely incredible man.

RD: He wrote: "The Christian religion is a parody on the worship of the sun, in which they put a man whom they called Christ in the place of the sun and pay him the same adoration which was originally paid to the sun." Why did you select Thomas Paine? And tell me more about this astro-theology.

JM: Because that is a classic comment about astro-theology. Astro-theology is the basis for all religion in the world, period.

RD: Astro, what does that mean?

JM: Astro-theology. Theology is the worship of a religion, and astro is the worship of the heavens. From as far back in history as we can go, man has always worshiped the heavens. That's why we're even told in western civilization that when you die, you'll go to heaven. And of course, the interesting point that Thomas Paine was making is the same one that I continue to make – that the whole concept of the son, S-O-N, God's son, goes directly back to the concept of God's sun, S-U-N, being the risen savior. Because the sun *is* the risen savior. It does rise. And according to the Egyptians, God's sun, S-U-N, had an evil brother, he was the prince of darkness. He came out at night to rule the world when God's sun died and went away, and the world was in hands of the prince of darkness. His name was Set, and he came out at sun-set. The Egyptians said that the newborn sun that came up every morning was Horus, and they would come out at the temples of Karnak and the temples at Thebes and Heliopolis in the morning (as they still do in the Islamic faith), and greet the coming of the new sun. We do it at Easter. We have Easter SUN-rise services.

RD: Horus-rising?

JM: Yes. Horus-risen. That's where we get the word "horizon." There are fifteen major religions in the world before Christianity that have taught the same thing. It is a very ancient story, coming from the greatest story ever told. I'm not saying there's not good spirituality in the Bible. I am saying it has been twisted and used by political powers for a political agenda to keep us ignorant, ill-informed, and unread. They keep most people dependent on the Lord to come back and help us, when in fact there is no Lord coming back at all. The keys are education, knowledge, and your own personal spirituality; and investigating what the story is really about. That's the only real salvation that we have left.

RD: Okay, but what about Adam and Eve? There's no Adam and Eve? What about Christ?

JM: No, that's why the Hebrews do not take part in Christianity. The Jews do not accept Jesus as the Messiah. Many Christians jump to the conclusion that the Jews don't accept Jesus because they hated the Messiah. No, no such thing is true. The reason why Jews do not accept Christianity is really rather simple. They know the story. And they know it's just a story. It's the gentiles that don't know this. What we need to do is wake up and find out that this is a story and what the story is telling us.

RD: Now, in our last discussion you were saying that the government talks about the separation of church and state, but that is not true.

JM: I don't believe that there's a separation.

RD: The government is very much involved with?...

JM: Religion. Yes. Actually, if you go back to the very beginnings of mankind there's always been this coexistence between government and religion, between church and state. And of course in all the ancient empires the king was also the mediator between god and man. So he wasn't just the king of the state, he was also the liaison between his people and God. Up until the time of the French Revolution, that was always the case, even in Europe, with the Papacy. Today, of course, we in America like to believe that we have a division between state and church, but it is my proposition, and my idea, that no such division exists. That the church as we know it today in western civilization, is nothing more than a tool and a counterpart to government. It is like two hands, government and religion, both helping the one mind to do its work. So that's what I'm intending to do – to enlighten people to where government, ideas, concepts, and belief systems have come from, and where theology and religion come from. I wish to show the connections behind the scenes of how we, because we're unread in the field, are being manipulated and exploited by government and religion. You asked me before what kind of reception I get. I get a very powerful positive response. When I was in New York, on ABC-New York with Bob Grant, I was supposed to do a half-hour program, but ended up doing a two-hour interview. The response was overwhelmingly positive. Many people in our country know instinctively that there's something going on in big government, big business, big money, and big religion. And everyone seems to know that, but no one as of yet has gone into and brought out the facts surrounding religion and government into our country, and the monetary connection.

RD: Okay, Jordan. So, what if people begin to see what you are saying, that the moral guidelines of our government are based on religion? Now, if you take away the religion, what will happen to the moral guidelines? We won't have any?

JM:Let's make a distinction here between religion and spirituality. I'm not talking about spirituality. That's something we need to keep. I'm a highly spiritual person. I believe in a divine God or creator, I am totally convinced that there is a divine essence to us, so I have no problem with spirituality.

RD: What makes you convinced that we do have a divine spirituality?

JM: Well, I think there are far too many things that happen to all human beings, that we know that there's more to life than just us. I think that all of us have had many experiences, every one of us, have had experiences that prove there is some sort of spiritual dynamic to our life. I myself have had many experiences in a spiritual way to convince me that I am not here on this earth by myself, and that there are spirits here. I believe in a God, or a creator. I don't have a problem with spirituality, I have a very big problem with government, money, and religion.

RD: Yes, it somewhat contaminates the beauty of the divine essence that is there.

JM: Absolutely. No doubt about it. We have the best politicians and religious leaders that money can buy, and I'm tired of that.

RD: Can I ask you something? Do you believe in reincarnation? And what does the Bible say about that?

JM: I think that you can make a good case for this, that there was much in the Old and New Testament to support reincarnation, but was taken out during the Middle Ages. We know that happened, we know that many scriptures were deleted, and some things were put in that were not in the original. So I think that the scriptures dealing with reincarnation were taken out purposely because the church felt that it would be harmful to the people, to think that they would come back, and that they come back again. Because if you keep coming back in other lifetimes, then why do you need to contribute to the church today? Why do you need to even go to church today, or even hear the priest, if you're going to come back the next time and do it over again anyway? So I think the church said no more of this, we have to take that out and let everyone believe that they have only one time through and that's it, so you have to be in subjection to religion.

RD: That right there shows the government being involved with church history.

JM: The history of Europe is filled with the Papacy and the Pope of Rome being involved with the kings and the princes of Europe. And, of course that is referred to as the "old" order of the world, the old world order. And in America we have our own religio-political foundations, and we call our ourselves a "new" world order, and that's even on the dollar bill. So there's a lot of connections behind the scenes between major religion, big money, and government. And that is what the book is about, *The Book Your Church Doesn't Want You To Read*. It's a general anthology on all the things in religion that the church doesn't want you to know about.

RD: Now, as we explore this, what happens to people as they become more enlightened?. I can not think of people never having a church in their life. Church seems to mean so much, and to give so much more to people. I mean, how would the church be changed? Would we ever have a church again?

JM: Did they have churches in Adam and Eve's day? I mean, when creation first began, with the ancient peoples in the ancient world, did they have churches? What I'm saying is there's a very big difference between religion, which requires a church, and the clergy, and money, and organization; as opposed to spirituality within your individual self, something spiritual between yourself and your divine creator. I don't believe there is a necessity for a church, synagogue, or whatever. I think that the spirituality is between you and your creator. So, I don't see a need for the church.

RD: I think I kind of pick up what your saying. Is that what you want – to bring back the essence and the innocence of people?

JM: Yes, absolutely.

RD: And not have all of this organized religion.

JM: And not have it function like entertainment, like Entertainment Tonight. I see nothing spiritual in church television and church radio, I see nothing more than Madison Avenue's promotion of religion that in all ways, and in every way, supports government.

RD: That would be a major metamorphosis for people.

JM: Yes.

RD: If that was to ever happen.

JM: I think that's going to happen. I think we are being forced, by events in the world, to wake up and begin to question our foundations and our belief systems. We expect the Arabs to do so, we expect the Hindus to examine their foundations and see that they need to explore what they believe. And it's very good for everyone else in the world to examine what they believe. Why isn't it good for us to do the same?

RD: So with Freemasonry, is that where symbolism started coming about?

JM: Yes, let me explain why I got into symbolism. As I mentioned earlier, my mother had an uncle who worked in the Vatican's Secretary of State's Office. Every few years he would come back and sit around for days, talking about all the intrigue that was going on behind the scenes of religion and politics. It was a very interesting conversation. And I would hear this kind of conversation where he would talk about symbols, emblems, secret societies, fraternal orders, and the wars and revolutions. In relation to the symbols, all of these emblems and symbols mean something, but so many people are unaware. I mean, the Bible has Jesus saying that many will look with their eyes but not see, and that is certainly true. People look at symbols all day long and have no idea in the world what they mean. Symbols are very important, and if you don't think so, watch someone wearing a swastika go into a synagogue and observe the reaction that the Jews will have when they see the swastika. This is because symbols mean something. They have very powerful meanings, but most of us are ignorant as to what most of these symbols are.

RD: I've often wondered about the swastika. Isn't it like a cross?

JM: Actually, it's originally Hindu. The swastika of Germany was a Hindu symbol, and then it generated down until finally the Nazis picked it up, like many other nations and peoples did. The American Indians and the Buddhists also use the swastika as a sacred symbol. I was also going to make mention of the foundations of western religion. We know that western religion is based on a far older Bible, the Bible of the Old Testament. Even further back, if you go back into the most ancient history of the world, especially in the Middle East, you will see that the volcano was one of the many things that was worshiped. The volcano was very important because it represented life and creation, and it had a sexual connotation.

RD: Wow.

JM: That's why today in most men's rooms, and hotels, and restaurants there will always be a triangle on the door. Triangle being the pyramid, or pyra-mid, coming from pyra, meaning fire, and mid, meaning middle. The fire of sexual generation is in the middle of the human body, that is why the volcano always represented sex, or the coming of life and the fire of life that brings new life to the world. So the volcano was a very important symbol to the ancient peoples of the world. The volcano, like any other impressive or fearful aspect of nature, had become an object of worship for human beings from the time of the earliest stone age. Yet the original Yahweh, which was one of the gods of the Old Testament, seems to have begun as a volcano god. Mount Sinai, where Moses encountered him, was the seat of the Middianite god, and in the Middianite's earliest homeland he was identified with the local Moon god "Sin," which is where we get the name for the mountain in the Middle East, Sin-ai, or Sinai. It comes from the old Moon god Sin, after whom the mountain was named. The Bible describes the appearance of Yahweh as a pillar of cloud by day and a pillar of fire by night, as found in Exodus 13: 21-22. The word volcano comes from the Latin volcano god Vulcan, or Vulcanus, derived from the old Cretan deity Velchanos. Now here we have the pillar of cloud by day, and the pillar of fire by night, and the Israelites in the desert with their representation of God.

In Job 38 we find that thunder, in Hebrew, is considered the voice of God. Thunder, in Hebrew, is called voices, or the voice of God. In other references on Job 38 it talks about the storm. It says that the storm and clouds are in God's tent, which gather as the thunder, as the voice of Yahweh. The voice of Yahweh is roaring, they descend and God shoots his arrows of lightning. So we're talking about the God of the Old Testament with his thunder and his arrows of lightning. In Hebrew, this reference states that "God thunders wonderfully with his voice." So now we see that thunder and lightning are connected to the old volcano god, the god of the volcano.

It is said that at Mount Sinai Jehovah performed signs, the mountain smoked and trembled all over, and many now heard the proof that what Moses had made known in God's name was actually the word of God. The Israelites were at Mount Sinai, which is always pictured time and again, in many biblical texts, as a volcano. Jehovah led the sons of Israel to the mountain named Sinai, and there he gave them his law. The mountain at Sinai where the Israelites encountered Yahweh was actually a volcano.

On the cover of the Jewish Torah we often see pictured the benediction symbol. This is the rabbinical benediction symbol that's the blessing symbol with which the rabbis bless the congregation. The high priest of Israel often raised his hands in the priestly blessing for Yahweh, the volcano god, or Vulcan. So we see that this is a priestly blessing in the Hebrew. And today the rabbi always gives the priestly blessing for Yahweh at the synagogue. This also explains why Mr. Spock from "Star Trek" gives the exact same "priestly blessing," and that's why Mr. Spock is called a Vulcan. That was the whole idea of the Vulcan, coming from Vulcanus, or the old Cretan deity which was later to be found in the Old Testament under the name of Yahweh.

So the point I'm making is that when we find the foundations for our religious movements in America and in Europe, then we find that from those religious foundations we have our political movements. And so therefore, what we need to do is understand that our religion and our politics are both one in the same. If we're under the law, and have to be a nation under the law, then the law is, of course, the law from the Old Testament volcano god. So, as I said, there are two kinds of facts in theology, the kind you look up, and the kind you make up. All I'm saying is that there's been a lot of theology that's been given to us, and we accept it blindly. But people still need to do their homework, because so much of what we've been given which is holy, turns out to be not so holy when you do your homework.

RD: Can I ask you one more thing? What about Noah and the Curse of Canaan?

JM: The Curse of Canaan (in Genesis 9:25) supposedly explains where the black man comes from, because he was cursed by God. That is a horrible misuse of scripture and I think it's too much of a subject to get into now. Suffice it to say that it was purposely used by people who knew better when they were using it, that it is not a curse on the black man. It has to do with the Curse on Canaan and the Canaanites, who were not black people. We can dispense with that, it was a misuse of scripture. When you get into Canaan and Babylon, one finds how even today, the Babylonian empire still affects our world. Many of our symbols and emblems come directly from Canaan and Babylon, so if there's a "Curse on Canaan," we're enjoying it right now.

RD: So, you don't feel that this is going to take anything away from people?

JM: No, I think it is a privilege to educate and help people to understand where things come from.

RD: To understand what's going on? Okay, I'm absolutely enthralled and I feel that it's such a treat that you've come to share this information with us.

The following interview with Jordan Maxwell was conducted by Ralph Walker.

RW: Let me introduce Jordan Maxwell.

JM: Secret societies are a very profound subject and it's one that most people haven't looked at very closely. For something that is so powerful and so important in our day, meaning the societies which control our country from behind the scenes, it's really important to understand how they got here and the symbols that are used. Occult symbols are like the letters of the alphabet, put them together and they tell a story. But if you can't read the symbols, you can't understand the story. A classic example I would like to bring to your audience's attention is on the dollar bill. Everyone has a one dollar bill in their pocket, but very few people have looked at the symbolism on the back. There's much talk in Washington today about a New World Order. If we look at the back of the dollar bill, on the left-hand side, we see the magic circle. Within that magic circle is the pyramid, with the all-seeing-eye separated above the top of the pyramid. Above the eye you have *Annuit Coeptis*. which is Latin for our enterprise (or project) is now a success.

RW: Now what was that enterprise?

JM: The enterprise itself is stated beneath the pyramid, *Novus Ordo Seclorum*, which is in Latin, *Novus* is for new, *Ordo* is for order, and *Seclorum* is for the secular, like your secular job, or your secular education, which means worldly, or the secular world. So the term means *New Order of the World*, or *The New World Order*.

RW: A term we hear quite frequently today.

JM: Exactly. Now the interesting thing about this symbol of the New World Order is why it's pictured beneath an Egyptian pyramid. Pyramids are in Egypt. So there's a reason why Egypt has played such a very big part in America. To the secret societies of the world, America is referred to as the "new Egypt," and therefore our symbols are from Egypt. Like in Washington, DC, where we have the obelisk and the White House. The obelisk is Cleopatra's Needle.

RW: Known as the Washington Monument.

JM: The Washington Monument is nothing more than the Egyptian Cleopatra's Needle. As a matter of fact, if you fly over Washington, DC and look down, or from pictures in a library of Washington, DC, from the air, you will see that it's laid out in a tremendous pyramid, with the Capitol Building in the triangle at the top.

The back of an American dollar bill showing the back and front (left and right, respectively) sides of the Great Seal of The United States.

There's the long waterway, that's the river Styx, which is out in front of Cleopatra's Needle and of course, at the end, is the magic circle, the Masonic circle. So it all has to do with ancient occult secret societies, fraternal orders, and their symbolism.

RW: A question that some viewers may be wondering is why it's written in Latin and not some African language?

JM: That a very good observation, because it is African symbolism, but Latin language. The new order was to be made up of an elitist society, but it was to be based on the old mysticism, religion, and philosophy of Africa, but it would be a new Africa, or a "new Egypt."

RW: So you're saying that modern society goes all the way back to the Great Pyramid.

JM: Oh yes, goes all the way back. As a matter of fact, if you remember, the pyramids are made out of bricks, and those who worked with bricks in the ancient world were called stone-masons, and today that's where we get the Masonic societies, or the Masons, who work with bricks. Almost all Freemasons realize that their fraternity of freemasonry goes all the way back into the ancient world, to the first dynasties of Egypt. Much of their symbolism comes from Egypt. It's important to understand that today, when the president talks about the New World Order, and you hear this term quite often now, that you understand what he's really saying. America is referred to as the New World, and of course, Christopher Columbus discovered the New World. The Old World is Europe and for almost 2,000 years Europe has controlled the world. Europe has dominated the world. And Rome has dominated Europe. So for almost 2,000 years Rome, or the Roman Church, the Roman authority of Europe, through their ancient and fraternal houses, have controlled Europe and Europe has dominated the world.

RW: Did The Crusades have anything to do with this?

JM: Absolutely, that's exactly right. That's why the Steven Spielberg and George Lucas movies, with Indiana Jones and the Last Crusade, should be of great interest to researchers. Of course, you can't understand the last crusade, if you don't know anything about the first one. It has to do with the lost ark, and that's why we have The Raiders of the Lost Ark, where they were searching for the Ark of the Covenant. It was purely an African symbol, which was later brought into modern use in the Bible, where it was referred to as the Ark of the Covenant. It actually comes from Egypt, it's a much older symbol.

But that's a whole different story. If you think about the power base in Europe being the old world, with those powers being behind the throne of Europe dominating the world, that was an order, like a Masonic order, or an order of priesthood – you know, the fraternal orders.

RW: Does that reflect on history, if several United States Presidents belong to the Masonic Order?

JM: Quite a few presidents did. In fact, many of the founders of the United States, the signers of the Constitution, were all Freemasons except for the few that were Rosicrucians, and there were a few others that were of other fraternal orders. In that respect, it's interesting to do a little research in your history books on an order called Prieure de Sion, the holy house of sion. That's S-I-O-N, not Z-I-O-N. It's a very powerful secret society that's even in existence in the south of France today. The south of France has always been a very mystical place for occult societies; for example, the Cathars, the Albigensians, and The Crusaders. Let me get back to this point about Rome dominating Europe, and Europe dominating the world. Rome, or the Roman Church today, was the power of Europe and that was the Old World Order. The order of the old world. But with the coming of America, we have a New World Order, and therefore the elite power-base which is America is the "new" order.

RW: Are you saying that power was passed on to America?

JM: That's right, the power was passed on to America.

RW: Or did they seize it and take it?

JM: They actually seized it, and took it, and moved the power base from Europe to America. And therefore, the order that is now directing affairs behind the scenes in America is referred to those on the "inside" as the New Order, the New World Order, because America is the New World. And when we understand the symbolism on the dollar bill, we catch only a glimpse of the whole picture. It's such an enormous subject, but many aspects can be seen in motion pictures and in Hollywood.

RW: We use this terminology "secret societies," but are they really secret?

JM: You see, not all of them are secret, many of them are semi-secret societies. In the 35 years that I've been interested in this subject, I've found that there's always going to be people who will come out of these societies, for whatever purpose, and for whatever reason, and begin to divulge some of the things that are going on behind the scenes. We sometimes hear about this from 50, to 60, to 100 years later when we find out that someone wrote a book, and then we look back and can see why things happened the way they did. And today, as a result of what's happened, our world is totally in the grips of secret societies. The Middle East is dominated by some very powerful secret societies and fraternal orders that are at work. That is why George Bush had the troops in the Middle East – it was to show power to other secret societies as to who is really in control of the Middle East.

RW: I want to ask a question for someone who may be out there. What about the Republican and Democratic Parties?

JM: I didn't write this, I'm just relating it to you – but George Washington mentioned in one of his letters, actually in two of his letters, to a reverend in 1794, that there was a secret society operating in Washington at the time. He referred to it as the Democratic Society, which was later to become known as the Democratic Party. He said that this society, the Democratic Society, or the Democratic Party, was, in his own words, a subversive movement within the republic. It had, and has, as its motive the dividing of the people from their government. To this day, you send your democratically elected leaders to Washington, not realizing that those elected leaders would be members of secret societies and fraternal orders that would be working in concert with the secret societies in Washington. You have to understand that Washington, DC is a very powerful spot in the world for secret activities.

RW: I'll throw out a name like Ross Perot.

JM: Well, Ross Perot is a newcomer; I go back into Woodrow Wilson's day – his connections with occult orders. He once said something of profound importance. He said, "Since I entered politics, I have chiefly had men's views confided to me privately. Some of the biggest men in the United States, in the field of commerce and manufacture, are afraid of something. They know that there is a power somewhere so organized, so subtle, so watchful, so interlocked, so complete, so pervasive, that they better not speak above their breath when they speak in condemnation of it." That is a word for word quote, from something called *The New Freedom* in 1913.

RW: What kind of symbolism can be found today from these occult orders?

JM: The first that comes to mind are the occult symbols on the dollar bill. There's an interesting point on the back of the dollar bill, on the right-hand side, with the eagle. Of course, the eagle is the old Phoenix symbol, of rising from the ashes of destruction. It comes from the old Roman symbols, which goes back even further than that. Above the eagle you'll see thirteen stars, just above the eagle's head. There are thirteen cloud-bursts around the thirteen stars, there are thirteen feathers along the wings, there are thirteen stripes in the shield, on one side there are thirteen arrows, on the other side there are thirteen leaves, and there are thirteen berries on the olive branch. The pyramid on the left-hand side of the dollar has thirteen layers.

RW: And what are the berries about?

JM: The most important thing is the number thirteen. Why is the number thirteen dominating the dollar bill? It's because thirteen is a very powerful mystical number to secret societies. Incidentally, why did we have thirteen colonies? Why didn't we have forty-two, or ten colonies, or one hundred and twenty-seven colonies? Why did we have thirteen?

RW: Now, people out there may say that thirteen is an unlucky number.

JM: That's right, thirteen's an unlucky number, for you! That's the point. Thirteen is unlucky for you to use because it's a holy number. The thirteen is based on Jesus, and his twelve apostles, making thirteen. The twelve followers of Jesus were called, in the Bible, the cornerstones of the New World. Jesus was twice referred to in the New Testament as the "chief cornerstone that the builder's rejected." The chief cornerstone! The word chief cornerstone in the Bible is a Greek word meaning the peak of a pyramid. That's what it means, so therefore the peak of a pyramid is a chief cornerstone. And according to the old cabalistic understanding of the Bible, the pyramid at the top (the capstone) is the eye of Jesus. The eye of Jesus. Let's look at that. The eye goes back to, of course, Horus, which was the Sun in ancient Egypt. And today we have that eye on the back of the dollar bill representing Jesus, or God's "son." There's a message there.

RW: Do you know the person who designed that symbol (on the back of the dollar bill)?

JM: I'm not sure who designed it originally, but that symbol, on the left hand side of the back of the dollar bill, was in existence, just as it is today, in Bavaria, in the south of Germany, in 1774. There was an organization, a secret society, a fraternal order called the Illuminati, which used that exact symbol as their trademark. You can still see it in European libraries and museums. The question is, how does it end up on an American dollar bill? Especially since it was from an old *German* secret society? That's the question. We then get into some of the fraternal orders that are behind the throne in America. This is such a vast subject.

RW: Which leads me to the next question. What is the impact of secret societies on American politics today.

JM: Secret societies are absolutely the heart, the blood, and the brains behind America today. People just don't see it. The Republican Party is one hand, the Democratic Party is another, and the brain is the secret societies behind the scenes. Very powerful and intelligent people are at work behind the scenes governing both the Democratic and Republican Parties. In point of fact, it doesn't matter who is made president, the power is always going to be in the hands of the people behind the scenes. That's why in America we have a right to elect. We love to talk about our right to elect, but we don't have the right to *select* – that is decided upon by those who are in power. Like today, Democrat Bill Clinton is a very well educated man, and he is a Rhodes Scholar. And if you understand where the Rhodes scholarship comes from, it's from Cecil Rhodes of South Africa. And Cecil Rhodes said, before he died, that he was going to leave his millions and millions of dollars to set up a secret society that would teach young white men to be able to come into power and handle the reins of a vast world government. So that was the dream of Cecil Rhodes, to be able to create a secret society that could dominate the world from behind the scenes – and do it with such expertise that no one would ever have knowledge about it.

RW: Now, it seems this could be happening. Do secret societies have any impact on the situation going on in Europe?

The White House, similar to England's White Hall, both being symbols of Freemasonic origin.

JM: Absolutely. Secret societies have something to do with everything that's going on in the entire world. You have to know that where there's politics, there is money. And where there's money and politics, there is religion. There are powerful forces at work right now in Yugoslavia. There were books written twenty years ago talking about how the secret societies in the early 1990s were going to break up Yugoslavia (and the Balkans), and they had already designed how they were going to do it, and who they were going to start the war with. Twenty years ago these books were written about Yugoslavia. That's just one example, and if you're into that type of research, you can pretty much tell what's coming down the line. You can already tell who's going to be doing what if you understand the story, as I said, if you can read the symbols.

RW: I know you're not just predicting doom out there. What can the American people do? Or people who want to change the situation, what can they do to expose these societies?

JM: Let me say this. I am directing my work, what I do, only to a select few – to those who really care about their lives, those who really care about the country they live in, those who really care about freedom and liberty. I believe that the most important thing that one can do is educate your mind first, because that's where real freedom is. It is in the intellect – it is spiritual and intellectual freedom. And without that kind of freedom, but with the things you don't understand, the things you don't know, and not being able to read symbols – that's where they have you, because you don't understand the game that's being played.

RW: We're in a world surrounded by fast moving symbols and images, and so no one takes the time to explore the history of these and see what they mean.

JM: Exactly.

RW: Now a question. You are very noted lecturer – are you going to be doing future events some time in the future?

JM: Yes, in fact I'm going to be doing some radio and TV programs. I did a two-hour show on ABC-New York and it was very exciting. We just did a TV program for CBS, I was on the CBS special "Ancient Mysteries of the Bible." I may be doing a program for NBC, that is hopefully in the works. And also, I've just done a number of radio programs here in Los Angeles.

RW: You're also going to do a book and lecture tour throughout southern California?

JM: Yes. There's an enormous amount of material. A lot of people might think that this is the kind of subject that, to know about, you'd have to be in government or behind the scenes. But you'd be surprised how much material is out there, if you just know where to look.

RW: Well, this is the information age and we're living in the information capital of the world, Los Angeles. I'm sure that most of the information that you've acquired you got right here in the United States.

JM: Oh sure, absolutely. You may be interested to know, however, who controls the flow of our *general* information, for the masses, beyond what people like you and I look for. Why is our country ruled from the District of Columbia, and why do we have the Columbia Broadcasting System (CBS), Columbia University, and of course the Space Shuttle Columbia? And of course, the Columbia Broadcasting System on television has the symbol of the all-seeing eye, the eye on the dollar bill. Let's notice the symbols, and read them. I know I'm repeating myself, but the United States is ruled from the White House, not the black house, or the brown house, but the White House. And England is, of course, ruled from the White Hall – which is like the Masonic hall, or the lodge hall. England's government comes from the White Hall, and America's from the White House. So there's symbols and emblems involved and they mean something. I want to point out something I consider very important. When the new King of England is crowned, when he is made King, listen to the words that the Arch Bishop of Canterbury will say to the new King in the initiation ceremony. He says that the King of England is taking this position as King for Jesus Christ, and ruling for Jehovah on God's throne. And that is why God's kingdom is represented by the United Kingdom. The United Kingdom is God's Kingdom. And of course Rome has a terrible dispute with that. Rome had (and has) a dispute with England being the center for God's kingdom, or the United Kingdom. The Pope always felt that he was the Vicar of Christ and that was the basis for two world wars, that we got involved in. It is being disputed as to who and what secret society is going to be dominating the world, the Old World of Rome, or the New World of Anglo-American. This is still being decided today, and upon that note I will conclude.

RW: Thank you, Jordan, for sharing so much of your important and fascinating knowledge.

JM: You're very welcome.

Tape Epilog: As you have seen, world politics is actually based on religion. A good place to begin your research would be *The History of the Christian Religion to the Year Two Hundred* by Charles Waite, and one of my favorite books entitled *Symbols, Sex, and the Stars* by Ernest Busenbark. Both of these books are available from The Book Tree, and I highly recommend them. I also encourage interested people who want more information to contact me directly, through the addresses, numbers, and/or web site provided in the front of this book.

ADDENDUM
Additional Quotes

The powers of financial capitalism had another far reaching aim, nothing less than to create a world system of financial control in pri-vate hands able to dominate the political system of each country and the economy of the world as a whole. This system was to be controlled in a feudalist fashion by the central banks of the world acting in con-cert, by secret agreements, arrived at in frequent private meetings and conferences. The apex of the system was the Bank for International Settlements in Basle, Switzerland, a private bank owned and con-trolled by the worlds' central banks which were themselves private corporations.

The growth of financial capitalism made possible a centralization of world economic control and use of this power for the direct benefit of financiers and the indirect injury of all other economic groups.

—Professor Carroll Quigley of Georgetown University, *Tragedy and Hope: A History of The World in Our Time* (Macmillan Company, 1966,)

The Council on Foreign Relations is "the establishment." Not only does it have influence and power in key decision-making positions at the highest levels of government to apply pressure from above, but it also announces and uses individuals and groups to bring pressure from below, to justify the high level decisions for converting the U.S. from a sovereign Constitutional Republic into a servile member state of a one-world dictatorship.

—Former Congressman John Rarick 1971

We are at present working discreetly with all our might to wrest this mysterious force called sovereignty out of the clutches of the local nation states of the world.

—Professor Arnold Toynbee, in a June 1931 speech before the Institute for the Study of International Affairs in Copenhagen.

If there are those who think we are to jump immediately into a new world order, actuated by complete understanding and brotherly love, they are doomed to disappointment. If we are ever to approach that time, it will be after patient and persistent effort of long duration. The present international situation of mistrust and fear can only be cor-rected by a formula of equal status, continuously applied, to every phase of international contacts, until the cobwebs of the old order are brushed out of the minds of the people of all lands.

—Dr. Augustus O. Thomas, president of the World Federation of Education Associations (August 1927), quoted in the book International Understanding: Agencies Educating for a New World (1931)

...when the struggle seems to be drifting definitely towards a world social democracy, there may still be very great delays and disap-pointments before it becomes an efficient and beneficent world sys-tem. Countless people... will hate the new world order... and will die protesting against it. When we attempt to evaluate its promise, we have to bear in mind the distress of a generation or so of malcontents, many of them quite gallant and graceful-looking people.

—H. G. Wells, in his book entitled The New World Order (1939)

99

The developing coherence of Asian regional thinking is reflected in a disposition to consider problems and loyalties in regional terms, and to evolve regional approaches to development needs and to the evolu - tion of a new world order.

—Richard Nixon, in Foreign Affairs (October 1967)

He [President Nixon] spoke of the talks as a beginning, saying noth - ing more about the prospects for future contacts and merely reiterat - ing the belief he brought to China that both nations share an interest in peace and building 'a new world order.

—Excerpt from an article in The New York Times (February 1972)

Further global progress is now possible only through a quest for uni - versal consensus in the movement towards a new world order.

—Mikhail Gorbachev, in an address at the United Nations (December 1988)

If we do not follow the dictates of our inner moral compass and stand up for human life, then his lawlessness will threaten the peace and democracy of the emerging new world order we now see, this long dreamed-of vision we've all worked toward for so long.

—President George Bush (January 1991)

But it became clear as time went on that in Mr. Bush's mind the New World Order was founded on a convergence of goals and interests between the U.S. and the Soviet Union, so strong and permanent that they would work as a team through the U.N. Security Council.

—Excerpt from A. M. Rosenthal, in The New York Times (January 1991)

... it's Bush's baby, even if he shares its popularization with Gorbachev. Forget the Hitler 'new order' root; F.D.R. used the phrase earlier.

—William Safire, in The New York Times (February 1991)

The new world order that is in the making must focus on the creation of a world of democracy, peace and prosperity for all.

—Nelson Mandela, in The Philadelphia Inquirer (October 1994)

The renewal of the nonproliferation treaty was described as important "for the welfare of the whole world and the new world order."

—President Hosni Mubarak of Egypt, in The New York Times (April 1995)

The New World Order will have to be built from the bottom up rather than from the top down. It will look like a great "booming, buzzing confusion," to use William James' famous description of reality, but an end run around national sovereignty, eroding it piece by piece, will accomplish much more than the old-fashioned frontal assault.

—CFR member Richard N. Gardner, writing in the April 1974 issue of the CFR's journal, Foreign Affairs.

Past Shock: The Origin of Religion and Its Impact on the Human Soul, **by Jack Barranger.** Twenty years ago, Alvin Toffler coined the term "future shock" — a syndrome in which people are overwhelmed by the future. *Past Shock* suggests that events that happened thousands of years ago very strongly impact humanity today. Technologically advanced beings created us as a slave race and in the process spiritually raped us.  This book reveals the real reasons why religion was created, what organized religion won't tell you, the reality of the "slave chip" programming we all have to deal with, why we had to be created over and over again, what really happened in the Garden of Eden, what the Tower of Babel was and the reason why we were stopped from building it, how we were conditioned to remain spiritually ignorant, and much more. Jack exposes what he calls the "pretender gods," advanced beings who were not divine, but had advanced knowledge of scientific principles which included genetic engineering. Our advanced science of today has unraveled their secrets, and people like Barranger have the knowledge and courage to expose exactly how we were manipulated. Learn about our past conditioning, and how to overcome the "slave chip" mentality to begin living life as it was meant to be, as a spiritually fulfilled being. **ISBN 1-885395-08-6 • 126 pages • 6 x 9 • trade paper • illustrated • $12.95**

Of Heaven and Earth: Essays Presented at the First Sitchin Studies Day, **edited by Zecharia Sitchin.** Zecharia Sitchin's previous books have sold millions around the world. This book, first published in 1996, contains further information on his incredible theories about the origins of mankind and the intervention by intelligences beyond the Earth. Sitchin, in previous works, offers the most scholarly and convincing approach to the ancient astronaut theory you will most certainly ever find. This book offers the complete transcript of the first Sitchin Studies Day, held in Denver, Colorado on Oct. 6, 1996. Zecharia Sitchin's keynote address opens the book, followed by six other prominent speakers whose work has been influenced by Sitchin. The other contributors to the book include two university professors, a clergyman, a UFO expert, a philosopher, and a novelist—who joined Zecharia Sitchin in Denver, Colorado, to describe how his findings and conclusions have affected what they teach and preach. They all seem to agree that the myths of ancient peoples were actual events as opposed to being figments of imaginations. Another point of agreement is in Sitchin's work being the early part of a new paradigm—one that is already beginning to shake the very foundations of religion, archaeology and our society in general. **ISBN 1-885395-17-5 • 164 pages • 5 1/2 x 8 1/2 • trade paper • illustrated • $14.95**

Space Travelers and the Genesis of the Human Form: Evidence of Intelligent Contact in the Solar System, **by Joan d'Arc.** Believers in extraterrestrial intelligent life (ETI) have no doubt been confronted with  the few standard arguments covered in this book that are pitched by most skeptics. But are they logical and internally consistent? Or are they based on mistaken assumptions, government-media hogwash, and outmoded scientific concepts? Even skeptics may want to explore the logical grounds upon which their staunch protest against the existence of ETI is founded. Can Darwinian evolution actually prove we are alone in the Universe? This book illustrates that Darwinian evolution is actually not an empirically predictable or testable scientific paradigm. Darwinian evolution is a circular argument which serves to keep Earth humans earthbound. The Space Travel Argument Against the Existence of ETI will be shown to be dependent on three factors: (1) the persistent imposition of Earth-centered technological constraints (specifically, rocket technology and radio signals) implying an anthropocentric "you can't get here from there" attitude; (2) mathematical logic deduced from the faulty linear notions of Darwinian evolution, which only serve to put the "cart before the horse"; and (3) a circular and untestable hypothesis which essentially states "they aren't here because they aren't here." This book also shows that ancient anthropomorphic artifacts on Mars and the Moon are evidence of "Game Wardens" in our own solar system. Could the Earth be a controlled DNA repository for the ongoing creation and dissemination of life forms, including humans. **ISBN 1-58509-127-8 • 208 pages • 6 x 9 • trade paper • illustrated • $18.95**

***Triumph of the Human Spirit: The Greatest Achievements of the Human Soul and How Its Power Can Change Your Life,* by Paul Tice.**  A triumph of the human spirit happens when we know we are right about something, put our heart into achieving its goal, and then succeed. There is no better feeling. People throughout history have triumphed while fighting for the highest ideal of all -- spiritual truth. Tice brings you back to relive and explore history's most incredible spiritual moments, bringing you into the lives of visionaries and great leaders who were in touch with their souls and followed their hearts. They explored God in their own way, exposed corruption and false teachings, or freed themselves and others from suppression. They were eliminated through violence, but on a spiritual level achieved victory because of their strong moral cause. Their spirit lives on, and the world was greatly improved. Tice covers other movements and people who may have physically failed, but spiritually triumphed. This book not only documents the history of spiritual giants, it shows how you can achieve your own spiritual triumph. In today's world we are free to explore the truth without fear of being tortured or executed. Various exercises will strengthen the soul and reveal its hidden power. One can discover their true spiritual source with this work and will be able to tap into it. This is the perfect book for all those who believe in spiritual freedom and have a passion for the truth. **ISBN 1-885395-57-4 · 295 pages · 6 x 9 · trade paper · illustrated · $19.95**

 ***That Old Time Religion: The Story of Religious Foundations,* by Jordan Maxwell and Paul Tice.** This book proves there is nothing new under the sun — including Christianity. It gives a complete rundown of the stellar, lunar, and solar evolution of our religious systems; contains new, long-awaited, exhaustive research on the gods and our beliefs; includes research by Dr. Alan A. Snow, famous Dead Sea Scrolls scholar, on astrology in the Dead Sea Scrolls. Dr. Snow has been referred to by Sydney Ohmarr as the "world's greatest authority on astrology and the Dead Sea Scrolls." Includes 3 chapters by Paul Tice, a well known Gnostic minister. This book is illustrated, organized, and very comprehensible. Educate yourself with clear documented proof, and be prepared to have your belief system shattered! **ISBN 1-58509-100-6 · 123 pages · 6 x 9 · trade paper · $13.95**

***Jumpin' Jehovah: Exposing the Atrocities of the Old Testament God,* by Paul Tice.** Was Jehovah a criminal? Was he psychotic? In the realm of the gods,  was Jehovah just a renegade punk gone wild? Paul Tice has collected all the dirt on this shady historical character. Once you read this book, your views on God will never be the same again. Jehovah is stripped bare of all his fabricated "godliness" and we discover in this book an entity with no sense of ethics, forgiveness or compassion. Jehovah delighted in roasting people alive and tormenting his followers in a variety of creative ways. Tice takes us from the very beginning, when this crafty character first came on the scene, and shows us how he conned and bullied his way to the top of the godly heap. Jehovah then maintained his standing through threats and coercion—and when that didn't work, he did what any mentally deranged god would do: he just moved in and killed people. Basic theological questions are explored like: Was Jehovah really a god, or a demon? Why did Jehovah never promise a heaven or any kind of reward to his followers? Does any entity who murders thousands of devoted followers deserve to be worshipped? What are the differences between a false god and a true one? Jehovah has stopped punishing people in terrible ways, so it's probably safe to buy this book. **ISBN 1-58509-102-2 · 103 pages · 6 x 9 · trade paper · $12.95**

 ***Mysteries Explored: The Search for Human Origins, UFOs, and Religious Beginnings,* by Jack Barranger and Paul Tice.** Jack Barranger and Paul Tice are two authors who have combined forces in an overall investigation into human origins, religion, mythology, UFOs, and other unexplained phenomena. In the first chapter, "The Legacy of Zecharia Sitchin", Barranger covers the importance of Sitchin's *Earth Chronicles* books, which is creating a revolution in the way we look at our past. In "The First Dragon" chapter, Tice examines the earliest known story containing dragons, coming from Sumerian/Babylonian mythology. In "Past Shock", Barranger suggests that events which happened thousands of years ago very strongly impact humanity today. In "UFOs: From Earth or Outer Space?" Tice explores the evidence for aliens being from other earthly dimensions as opposed to having an extraterrestrial origin. "Is Religion Harmful?" looks at the origins of religion and why the entire idea may no longer be working for us, while "A Call to Heresy" shows how Jesus and the Buddha were considered heretics in their day, and how we have reached a critical point in our present spiritual development that requires another such leap. Aside from these chapters, the book also contains a number of outrageous (but discontinued) newsletters, including: Promethean Fire, Pleiadian Poop, and Intrusions. **ISBN 1-58509-101-4 · 103 pages · 6 x 9 · trade paper · $12.95**

Of Heaven and Earth: Essays Presented at the First Sitchin Studies Day, edited by Zecharia Sitchin. ISBN 1-885395-17-5 • 164 pages • 5 1/2 x 8 1/2 • trade paper • illustrated • $14.95

God Games: What Do You Do Forever?, by Neil Freer. ISBN 1-885395-39-6 • 312 pages • 6 x 9 • trade paper • $19.95

Space Travelers and the Genesis of the Human Form: Evidence of Intelligent Contact in the Solar System, by Joan d'Arc. ISBN 1-58509-127-8 • 208 pages • 6 x 9 • trade paper • illustrated • $18.95

Humanity's Extraterrestrial Origins: ET Influences on Humankind's Biological and Cultural Evolution, by Dr. Arthur David Horn with Lynette Mallory-Horn. ISBN 3-931652-31-9 • 373 pages • 6 x 9 • trade paper • $17.00

Past Shock: The Origin of Religion and Its Impact on the Human Soul, by Jack Barranger. ISBN 1-885395-08-6 • 126 pages • 6 x 9 • trade paper • illustrated • $12.95

Flying Serpents and Dragons: The Story of Mankind's Reptilian Past, by R.A. Boulay. ISBN 1-885395-38-8 • 276 pages • 6 x 9 • trade paper • illustrated • $19.95

Triumph of the Human Spirit: The Greatest Achievements of the Human Soul and How Its Power Can Change Your Life, by Paul Tice. ISBN 1-885395-57-4 • 295 pages • 6 x 9 • trade paper • illustrated • $19.95

Mysteries Explored: The Search for Human Origins, UFOs, and Religious Beginnings, by Jack Barranger and Paul Tice. ISBN 1-58509-101-4 • 104 pages • 6 x 9 • trade paper • $12.95

Mushrooms and Mankind: The Impact of Mushrooms on Human Consciousness and Religion, by James Arthur. ISBN 1-58509-151-0 • 103 pages • 6 x 9 • trade paper • $12.95

Vril or Vital Magnetism, with an Introduction by Paul Tice. ISBN 1-58509-030-1 • 124 pages • 5 1/2 x 8 1/2 • trade paper • $12.95

The Odic Force: Letters on Od and Magnetism, by Karl von Reichenbach. ISBN 1-58509-001-8 • 192 pages • 6 x 9 • trade paper • $15.95

The New Revelation: The Coming of a New Spiritual Paradigm, by Arthur Conan Doyle. ISBN 1-58509-220-7 • 124 pages • 6 x 9 • trade paper • $12.95

The Astral World: Its Scenes, Dwellers, and Phenomena, by Swami Panchadasi.ISBN 1-58509-071-9 • 104 pages • 6 x 9 • trade paper • $11.95

Reason and Belief: The Impact of Scientific Discovery on Religious and Spiritual Faith, by Sir Oliver Lodge. ISBN 1-58509-226-6 • 180 pages • 6 x 9 • trade paper • $17.95

William Blake: A Biography, by Basil De Selincourt. ISBN 1-58509-225-8 • 384 pages • 6 x 9 • trade paper • $28.95

The Divine Pymander: And Other Writings of Hermes Trismegistus, translated by John D. Chambers. ISBN 1-58509-046-8 • 196 pages • 6 x 9 • trade paper • $16.95

Theosophy and The Secret Doctrine, by Harriet L. Henderson. Includes **H.P. Blavatsky: An Outline of Her Life,** by Herbert Whyte, ISBN 1-58509-075-1 • 132 pages • 6 x 9 • trade paper • $13.95

The Light of Egypt, Volume One: The Science of the Soul and the Stars, by Thomas H. Burgoyne. ISBN 1-58509-051-4 • 320 pages • 6 x 9 • trade paper • illustrated • $24.95

The Light of Egypt, Volume Two: The Science of the Soul and the Stars, by Thomas H. Burgoyne. ISBN 1-58509-052-2 • 224 pages • 6 x 9 • trade paper • illustrated • $17.95

The Jumping Frog and 18 Other Stories: 19 Unforgettable Mark Twain Stories, by Mark Twain. ISBN 1-58509-200-2 • 128 pages • 6 x 9 • trade paper • $12.95

The Devil's Dictionary: A Guidebook for Cynics, by Ambrose Bierce. ISBN 1-58509-016-6 • 144 pages • 6 x 9 • trade paper • $12.95

The Smoky God: Or The Voyage to the Inner World, by Willis George Emerson. ISBN 1-58509-067-0 • 184 pages • 6 x 9 • trade paper • illustrated • $15.95

A Short History of the World, by H.G. Wells.ISBN 1-58509-211-8 • 320 pages • 6 x 9 • trade paper • $24.95

The Voyages and Discoveries of the Companions of Columbus, by Washington Irving. ISBN 1-58509-500-1 • 352 pages • 6 x 9 • hard cover • $39.95

History of Baalbek, by Michel Alouf. ISBN 1-58509-063-8 • 196 pages • 5 x 8 • trade paper • illustrated • $15.95

Ancient Egyptian Masonry: The Building Craft, by Sommers Clarke and R. Engelback. ISBN 1-58509-059-X • 350 pages • 6 x 9 • trade paper • illustrated • $26.95

That Old Time Religion: The Story of Religious Foundations, by Jordan Maxwell and Paul Tice. ISBN 1-58509-100-6 • 123 pages • 6 x 9 • trade paper • $13.95

Jumpin' Jehovah: Exposing the Atrocities of the Old Testament God, by Paul Tice. ISBN 1-58509-102-2 • 103 pages • 6 x 9 • trade paper • $12.95

The Book of Enoch: A Work of Visionary Revelation and Prophecy, Revealing Divine Secrets and Fantastic Information about Creation, Salvation, Heaven and Hell, translated by R. H. Charles. ISBN 1-58509-019-0 • 152 pages • 5 1/2 x 8 1/2 • trade paper • $13.95

The Book of Enoch: Translated from the Editor's Ethiopic Text and Edited with an Enlarged Introduction, Notes and Indexes, Together with a Reprint of the Greek Fragments, edited by R. H. Charles. ISBN 1-58509-080-8 • 448 pages • 6 x 9 • trade paper • $34.95

The Book of the Secrets of Enoch, translated from the Slavonic by W. R. Morfill. Edited, with Introduction and Notes by R. H. Charles. ISBN 1-58509-020-4 • 148 pages • 5 1/2 x 8 1/2 • trade paper • $13.95

Enuma Elish: The Seven Tablets of Creation, Volume One, by L. W. King. ISBN 1-58509-041-7 • 236 pages • 6 x 9 • trade paper • illustrated • $18.95

Enuma Elish: The Seven Tablets of Creation, Volume Two, by L. W. King. ISBN 1-58509-042-5 • 260 pages • 6 x 9 • trade paper • illustrated • $19.95

Enuma Elish, Volumes One and Two: The Seven Tablets of Creation, by L. W. King. Two volumes from above bound as one. ISBN 1-58509-043-3 • 496 pages • 6 x 9 • trade paper • illustrated • $38.90

The Archko Volume: Documents that Claim Proof to the Life, Death, and Resurrection of Christ, by Drs. McIntosh and Twyman. ISBN 1-58509-082-4 • 248 pages • 6 x 9 • trade paper • $20.95

The Lost Language of Symbolism: An Inquiry into the Origin of Certain Letters, Words, Names, Fairy-Tales, Folklore, and Mythologies, by Harold Bayley. ISBN 1-58509-070-0 • 384 pages • 6 x 9 • trade paper • $27.95

The Book of Jasher: A Suppressed Book that was Removed from the Bible, Referred to in Joshua and Second Samuel, translated by Albinus Alcuin (800 AD). ISBN 1-58509-081-6 • 304 pages • 6 x 9 • trade paper • $24.95

The Bible's Most Embarrassing Moments, with an Introduction by Paul Tice. ISBN 1-58509-025-5 • 172 pages • 5 x 8 • trade paper • $14.95

History of the Cross: The Pagan Origin and Idolatrous Adoption and Worship of the Image, by Henry Dana Ward. ISBN 1-58509-056-5 • 104 pages • 6 x 9 • trade paper • illustrated • $11.95

Was Jesus Influenced by Buddhism? A Comparative Study of the Lives and Thoughts of Gautama and Jesus, by Dwight Goddard. ISBN 1-58509-027-1 • 252 pages • 6 x 9 • trade paper • $19.95

History of the Christian Religion to the Year Two Hundred, by Charles B. Waite. ISBN 1-885395-15-9 • 556 pages. • 6 x 9 • hard cover • $25.00

Symbols, Sex, and the Stars, by Ernest Busenbark.ISBN 1-885395-19-1 • 396 pages • 5 1/2 x 8 1/2 • trade paper • $22.95

History of the First Council of Nice: A World's Christian Convention, A.D. 325, by Dean Dudley. ISBN 1-58509-023-9 • 132 pages • 5 1/2 x 8 1/2 • trade paper • $12.95

The World's Sixteen Crucified Saviors, by Kersey Graves. ISBN 1-58509-018-2 • 436 pages • 5 1/2 x 8 1/2 • trade paper • $29.95

Babylonian Influence on the Bible and Popular Beliefs: A Comparative Study of Genesis 1.2, by A. Smythe Palmer. ISBN 1-58509-000-X • 124 pages • 6 x 9 • trade paper • $12.95

Biography of Satan: Exposing the Origins of the Devil, by Kersey Graves. ISBN 1-885395-11-6 • 168 pages • 5 1/2 x 8 1/2 • trade paper • $13.95

The Malleus Maleficarum: The Notorious Handbook Once Used to Condemn and Punish "Witches", by Heinrich Kramer and James Sprenger. ISBN 1-58509-098-0 • 332 pages • 6 x 9 • trade paper • $25.95

Crux Ansata: An Indictment of the Roman Catholic Church, by H. G. Wells. ISBN 1-58509-210-X • 160 pages • 6 x 9 • trade paper • $14.95

Emanuel Swedenborg: The Spiritual Columbus, by U.S.E. (William Spear). ISBN 1-58509-096-4 • 208 pages • 6 x 9 • trade paper • $17.95

Dragons and Dragon Lore, by Ernest Ingersoll. ISBN 1-58509-021-2 • 228 pages • 6 x 9 • trade paper • illustrated • $17.95

The Vision of God, by Nicholas of Cusa. ISBN 1-58509-004-2 • 160 pages • 5 x 8 • trade paper • $13.95

The Historical Jesus and the Mythical Christ: Separating Fact From Fiction, by Gerald Massey. ISBN 1-58509-073-5 • 244 pages • 6 x 9 • trade paper • $18.95

Gog and Magog: The Giants in Guildhall; Their Real and Legendary History, with an Account of Other Giants at Home and Abroad, by F.W. Fairholt. ISBN 1-58509-084-0 • 172 pages • 6 x 9 • trade paper • $16.95

The Origin and Evolution of Religion, by Albert Churchward. ISBN 1-58509-078-6 • 504 pages • 6 x 9 • trade paper • $39.95

The Origin of Biblical Traditions, by Albert T. Clay. ISBN 1-58509-065-4 • 220 pages • 5 1/2 x 8 1/2 • trade paper • $17.95

Aryan Sun Myths, by Sarah Elizabeth Titcomb, Introduction by Charles Morris.ISBN 1-58509-069-7 • 192 pages • 6 x 9 • trade paper • $15.95

The Social Record of Christianity, by Joseph McCabe. Includes **The Lies and Fallacies of the Encyclopedia Britannica,** ISBN 1-58509-215-0 • 204 pages • 6 x 9 • trade paper • $17.95

The History of the Christian Religion and Church During the First Three Centuries, by Dr. Augustus Neander. ISBN 1-58509-077-8 • 112 pages • 6 x 9 • trade paper • $12.95

Ancient Symbol Worship: Influence of the Phallic Idea in the Religions of Antiquity, by Hodder M. Westropp and C. Staniland Wake. ISBN 1-58509-048-4 • 120 pages • 6 x 9 • trade paper • illustrated • $12.95

The Gnosis: Or Ancient Wisdom in the Christian Scriptures, by William Kingsland. ISBN 1-58509-047-6 • 232 pages • 6 x 9 • trade paper • $18.95

The Evolution of the Idea of God: An Inquiry into the Origin of Religions, by Grant Allen. ISBN 1-58509-074-3 • 160 pages • 6 x 9 • trade paper • $14.95

Sun Lore of All Ages: A Survey of Solar Mythology, Folklore, Customs, Worship, Festivals, and Superstition, by William Tyler Olcott. ISBN 1-58509-044-1 • 316 pages • 6 x 9 • trade paper • $24.95

Nature Worship: An Account of Phallic Faiths and Practices Ancient and Modern, by the Author of Phallicism with an Introduction by Tedd St. Rain. ISBN 1-58509-049-2 • 112 pages • 6 x 9 • trade paper • illustrated • $12.95

Life and Religion, by Max Muller. ISBN 1-885395-10-8 • 237 pages • 5 1/2 x 8 1/2 • trade paper • $14.95

Jesus: God, Man, or Myth? An Examination of the Evidence, by Herbert Cutner. ISBN 1-58509-072-7 • 304 pages • 6 x 9 • trade paper • $23.95

Pagan and Christian Creeds: Their Origin and Meaning, by Edward Carpenter. ISBN 1-58509-024-7 • 316 pages • 5 1/2 x 8 1/2 • trade paper • $24.95

The Christ Myth: A Study, by Elizabeth Evans. ISBN 1-58509-037-9 • 136 pages • 6 x 9 • trade paper • $13.95

Popery: Foe of the Church and the Republic, by Joseph F. Van Dyke. ISBN 1-58509-058-1 • 336 pages • 6 x 9 • trade paper • illustrated • $25.95

Career of Religious Ideas, by Hudson Tuttle. ISBN 1-58509-066-2 • 172 pages • 5 x 8 • trade paper • $15.95

Buddhist Suttas: Major Scriptural Writings from Early Buddhism, by T.W. Rhys Davids. ISBN 1-58509-079-4 • 376 pages • 6 x 9 • trade paper • $27.95

Early Buddhism, by T. W. Rhys Davids. Includes *Buddhist Ethics: The Way to Salvation?,* by Paul Tice. ISBN 1-58509-076-X • 112 pages • 6 x 9 • trade paper • $12.95

The Fountain-Head of Religion: A Comparative Study of the Principal Religions of the World and a Manifestation of their Common Origin from the Vedas, by Ganga Prasad. ISBN 1-58509-054-9 • 276 pages • 6 x 9 • trade paper • $22.95

India: What Can It Teach Us?, by Max Muller. ISBN 1-58509-064-6 • 284 pages • 5 1/2 x 8 1/2 • trade paper • $22.95

Matrix of Power: How the World has Been Controlled by Powerful People Without Your Knowledge, by Jordan Maxwell. ISBN 1-58509-120-0 • 103 pages • 6 x 9 • trade paper • $12.95

Cyberculture Counterconspiracy: A Steamshovel Web Reader, Volume One, edited by Kenn Thomas. ISBN 1-58509-125-1 • 180 pages • 6 x 9 • trade paper • illustrated • $16.95

Cyberculture Counterconspiracy: A Steamshovel Web Reader, Volume Two, edited by Kenn Thomas. ISBN 1-58509-126-X • 132 pages • 6 x 9 • trade paper • illustrated • $13.95

Oklahoma City Bombing: The Suppressed Truth, by Jon Rappoport. ISBN 1-885395-22-1 • 112 pages • 5 1/2 x 8 1/2 • trade paper • $12.95

The Protocols of the Learned Elders of Zion, by Victor Marsden. ISBN 1-58509-015-8 • 312 pages • 6 x 9 • trade paper • $24.95

Secret Societies and Subversive Movements, by Nesta H. Webster. ISBN 1-58509-092-1 • 432 pages • 6 x 9 • trade paper • $29.95

The Secret Doctrine of the Rosicrucians, by Magus Incognito. ISBN 1-58509-091-3 • 256 pages • 6 x 9 • trade paper • $20.95

The Origin and Evolution of Freemasonry: Connected with the Origin and Evolution of the Human Race, by Albert Churchward. ISBN 1-58509-029-8 • 240 pages • 6 x 9 • trade paper • $18.95

The Lost Key: An Explanation and Application of Masonic Symbols, by Prentiss Tucker. ISBN 1-58509-050-6 • 192 pages • 6 x 9 • trade paper • illustrated • $15.95

The Character, Claims, and Practical Workings of Freemasonry, by Rev. C.G. Finney. ISBN 1-58509-094-8 • 288 pages • 6 x 9 • trade paper • $22.95

The Secret World Government or "The Hidden Hand": The Unrevealed in History, by Maj.-Gen., Count Cherep-Spiridovich. ISBN 1-58509-093-X • 203 pages • 6 x 9 • trade paper • $17.95

The Magus, Book One: A Complete System of Occult Philosophy, by Francis Barrett. ISBN 1-58509-031-X • 200 pages • 6 x 9 • trade paper • illustrated • $16.95

The Magus, Book Two: A Complete System of Occult Philosophy, by Francis Barrett. ISBN 1-58509-032-8 • 220 pages • 6 x 9 • trade paper • illustrated • $17.95

The Magus, Book One and Two: A Complete System of Occult Philosophy, by Francis Barrett. ISBN 1-58509-033-6 • 420 pages • 6 x 9 • trade paper • illustrated • $34.90

The Key of Solomon The King, by S. Liddell MacGregor Mathers. ISBN 1-58509-022-0 • 152 pages • 6 x 9 • trade paper • illustrated • $12.95

Magic and Mystery in Tibet, by Alexandra David-Neel. ISBN 1-58509-097-2 • 352 pages • 6 x 9 • trade paper • $26.95

The Comte de St. Germain, by I. Cooper Oakley. ISBN 1-58509-068-9 • 280 pages • 6 x 9 • trade paper • illustrated • $22.95

Alchemy Rediscovered and Restored, by A. Cockren. ISBN 1-58509-028-X • 156 pages • 5 1/2 x 8 1/2 • trade paper • $13.95

The 6th and 7th Books of Moses, with an Introduction by Paul Tice. ISBN 1-58509-045-X • 188 pages • 6 x 9 • trade paper • illustrated • $16.95

CPSIA information can be obtained
at www.ICGtesting.com
Printed in the USA
LVHW032241131221
706134LV00014B/162